Museum of Lisbon
highlights

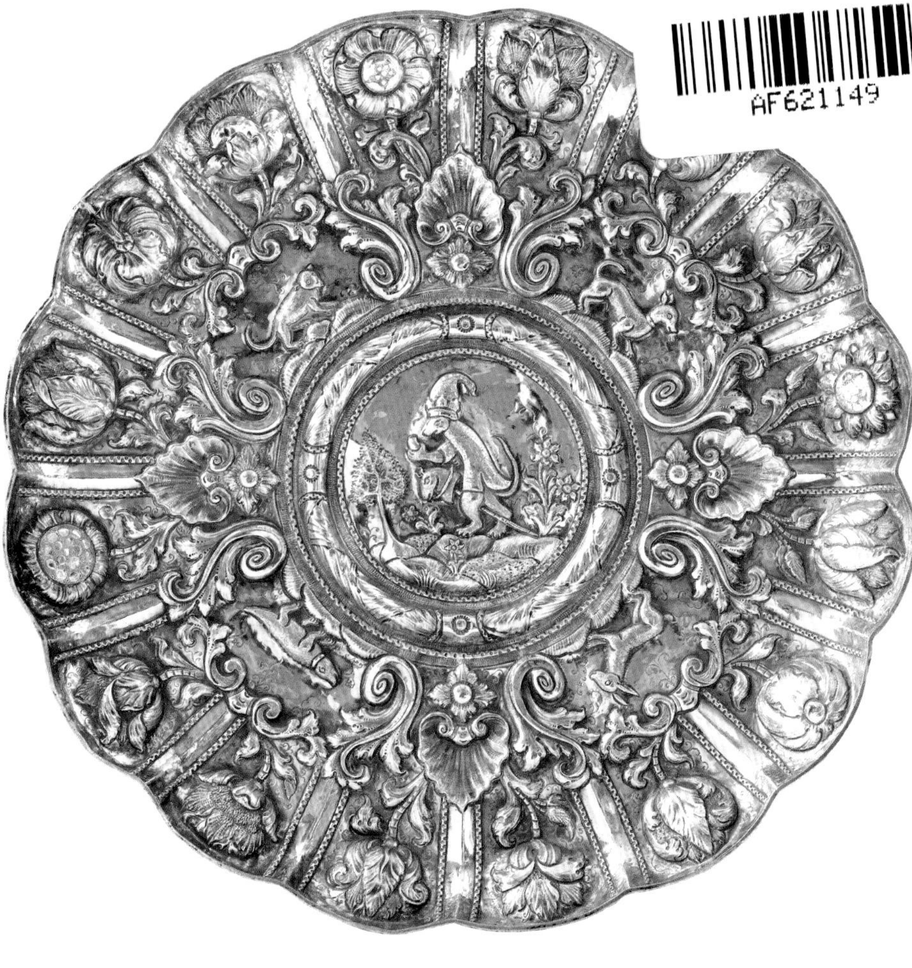

SCALA

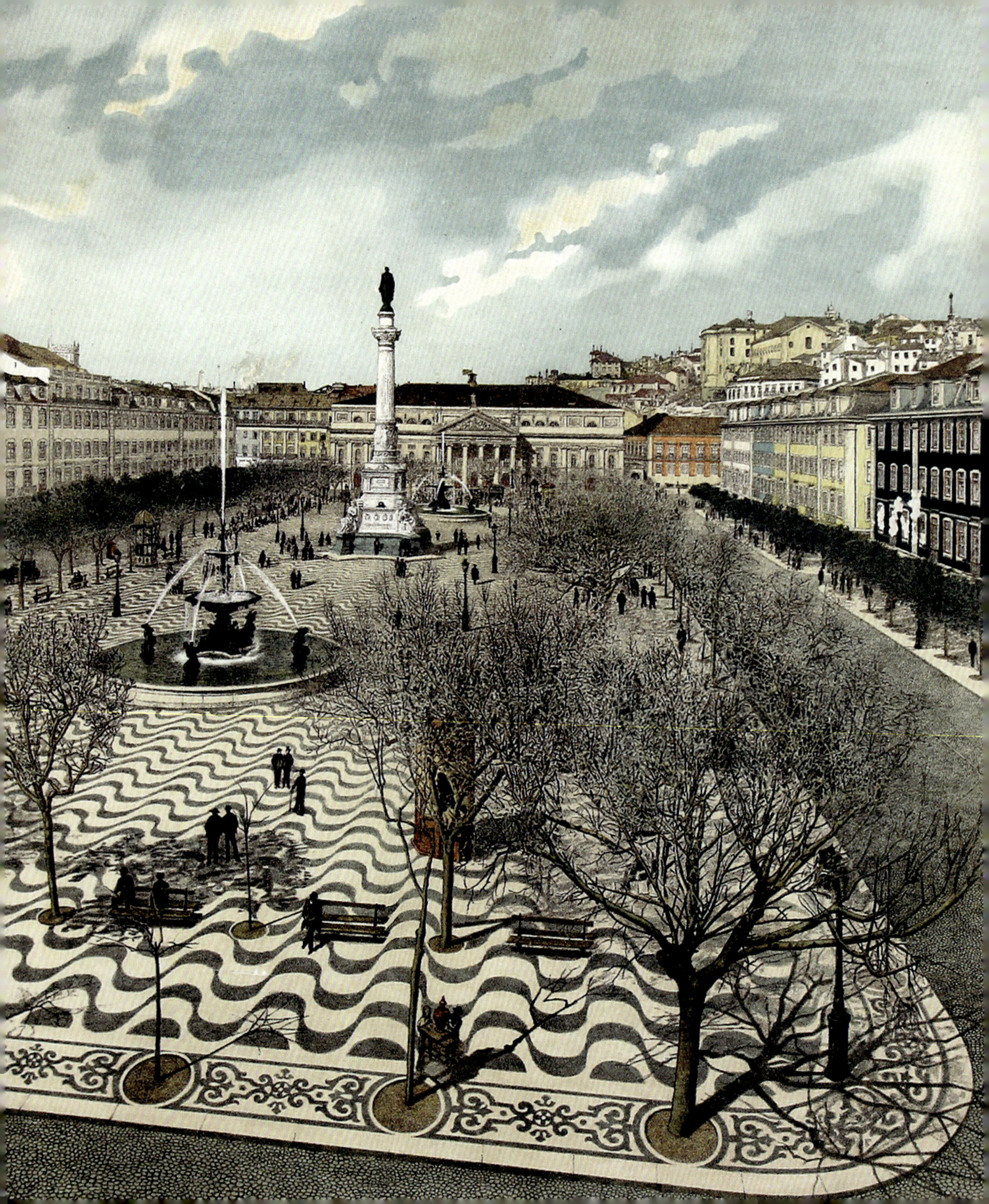

CONTENTS

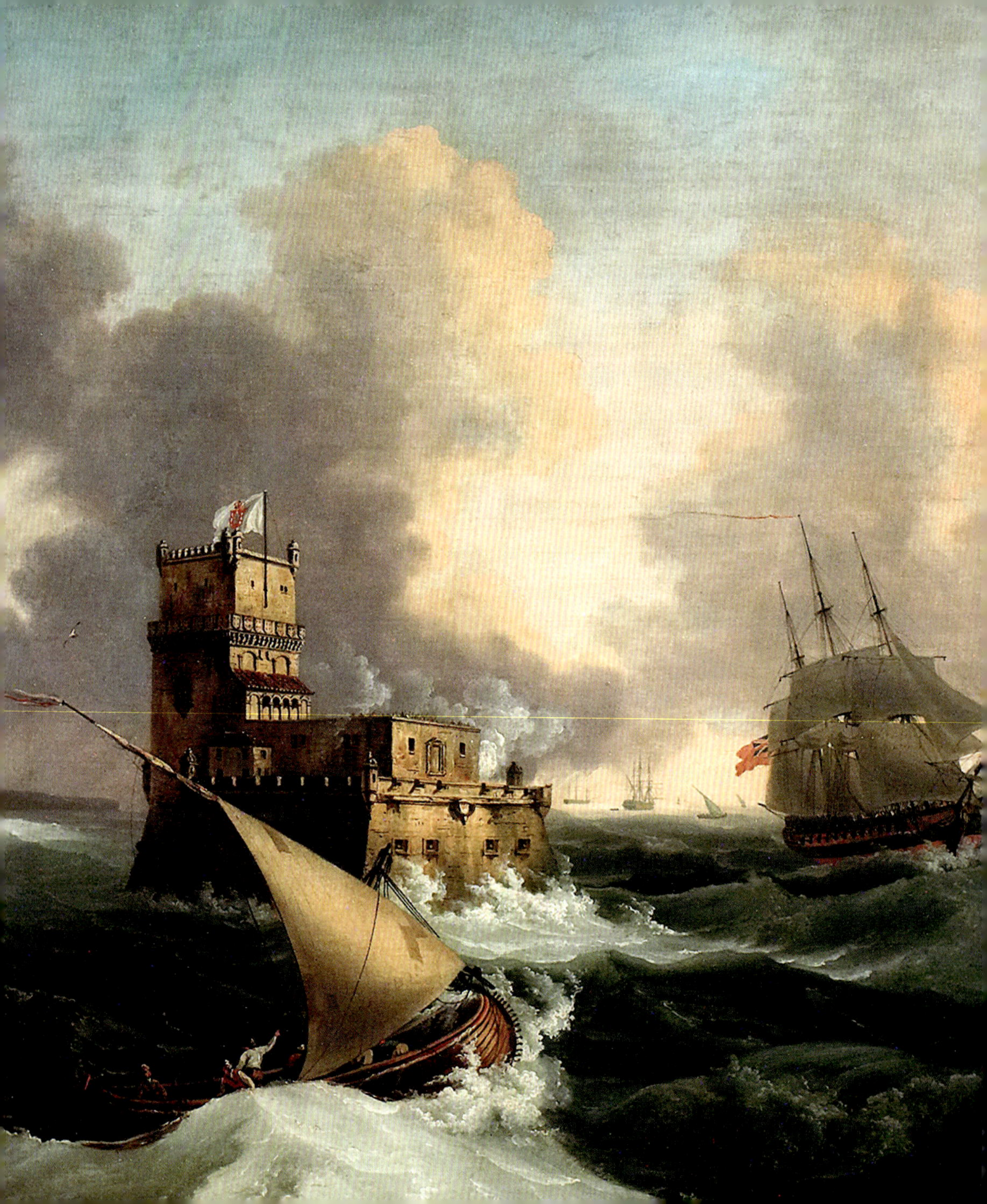

FOREWORD

Welcome to the Museum of Lisbon.

It is with great pleasure that we invite you to discover Lisbon through the eyes of our museum. Before starting our journey through the 2,000 and more years of the city's history, we would like to share with you what the museum is about.

The Museum of Lisbon's purpose is to explore, interpret and inform visitors about the extraordinary city that Lisbon has been ever since it was called Olisipo during the Roman era. Through the exhibitions and the large number of activities that we host in various places around the city, you will be awe-struck by the immense richness of stories, heritage and cultures that once belonged, and still do, to the people of Lisbon.

Our museum introduces you to Lisbon's Roman Theatre, and, through it, to a wealth of information about what the Roman city was like. The part of the museum dedicated to St Anthony shines a light on the medieval city and the strength of its folk traditions. You will also encounter the extraordinary episode – in every sense – that was the earthquake in 1755, and the rebuilding, masterminded by the Marquis of Pombal, that inspired other cities around the world. And you can see the changes to the layout of the city that occurred with the establishment of the Republic all the way to the April Revolution and Expo '98.

To us, Lisbon is one of the world's most beautiful and interesting cities. We hope that we can inspire you to feel the same way about it through our museum and the highlights presented in this book.

Joana Sousa Monteiro, Director of the Museum of Lisbon

ACKNOWLEDGEMENTS
We would like to thank Paulo Almeida Fernandes, José Avelar (photography), Lídia Fernandes (the Roman Theatre), Cristóvão Fonseca (the Roman Theatre), Maria de Lurdes Batista, Catarina Santiago Costa and Pedro Teotónio Pereira (Saint Anthony).

A MULTI-BRANCHED MUSEUM FOR A MULTI-FACETED CITY

The Museum of Lisbon explores the rich and diverse history of one of the oldest cities in Europe. It is set in five locations – Pimenta Palace, Saint Anthony, the Roman Theatre, the archaeological site of Casa dos Bicos and the West Tower of Praça do Comércio – each site covering a complementary aspect of the city's history.

Pimenta Palace

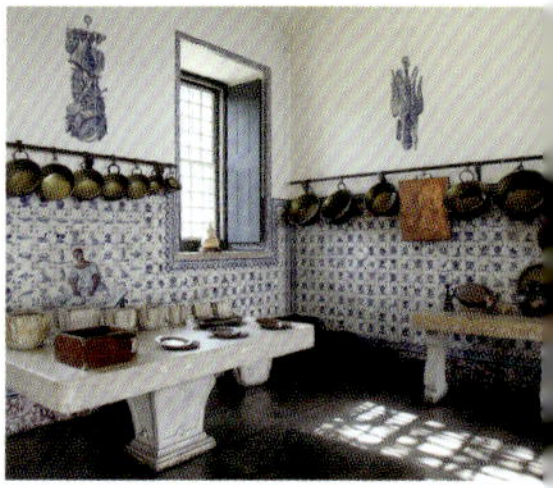

The principal site of the Museum is Pimenta Palace, a summer residence commissioned by Diogo de Sousa Mexia and built between 1734 and 1746. The building had several owners over the centuries and in 1833 it was bought by Manuel Joaquim Pimenta, hence its current name. In 1962 it was purchased by Lisbon Council to rehouse the city's museum and was opened to the public at this new site in 1979.

Saint Anthony

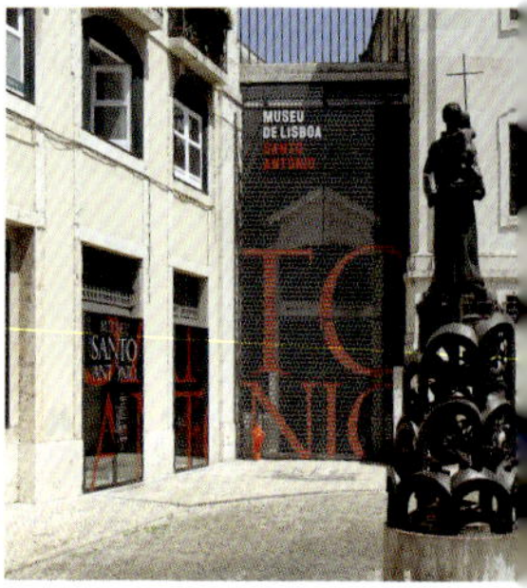

This branch of the Museum is dedicated to the life of St Anthony, an important figure in Portugal and in countries of the former Portuguese empire. St Anthony was born near the cathedral in Lisbon around 1191 and died in Arcela (near the Italian city of Padua) in 1231. The austere image of the only Portuguese Doctor of the Church gradually gave way to the popular one of Santo Antoninho (a diminutive of António) by which he is also known today. Devotees prayed to the popular saint for help with problems of all kinds. The date of his death, 13 June, is a public holiday in Lisbon.

Roman Theatre

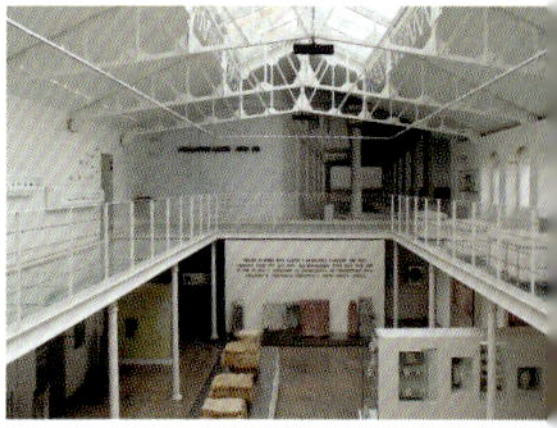

Discovered in 1798, when Lisbon was being rebuilt after the 1755 earthquake, the Roman Theatre was first excavated in 1964, and archaeological research continues to this day. It was built in the first century AD, its semi-circular structure adapted to the hillside. It was a theatre of considerable size, seating around 4,000 spectators.

Casa dos Bicos archaeological site

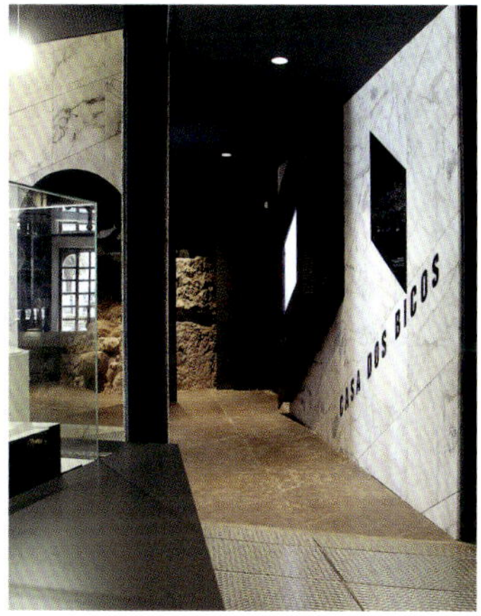

Located in the riverside area of the city and inaugurated on 14 July 2014, this archaeological site is housed in one of the most representative examples of sixteenth-century civic architecture in Lisbon. It was built by Brás de Albuquerque, the son of Afonso de Albuquerque, first viceroy of Portuguese India. The upper floors of the house are occupied by the José Saramago Foundation, whilst the ground floor, as part of the Museum of Lisbon, houses an exhibition charting 2,000 years of the city's history. Artefacts include parts of the Roman city wall of Lisbon and *cetaria* (fish-salting tanks) from a Roman factory which made fish preserves and sauces, mainly for exportation.

West Tower of Praça do Comércio

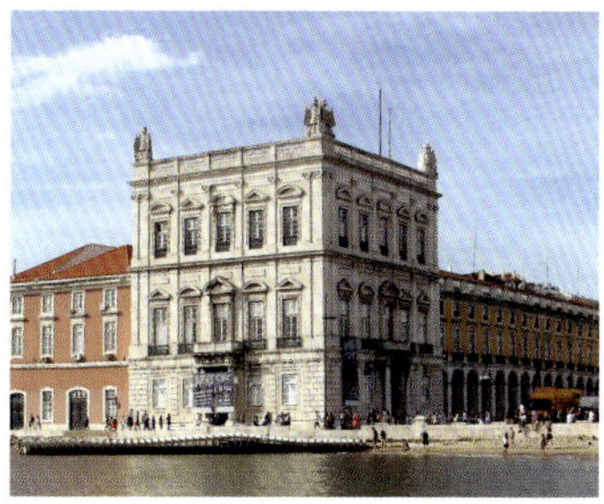

Although a nineteenth-century structure, the West Tower is part of the set of buildings that form Praça do Comércio, which replaced Terreiro do Paço after the earthquake in 1755. The Tower is situated in the approximate location of the former riverside royal palace (Paço da Ribeira). It holds temporary and medium-term exhibitions on a variety of subjects related to Lisbon's past and present.

Roman Galleries

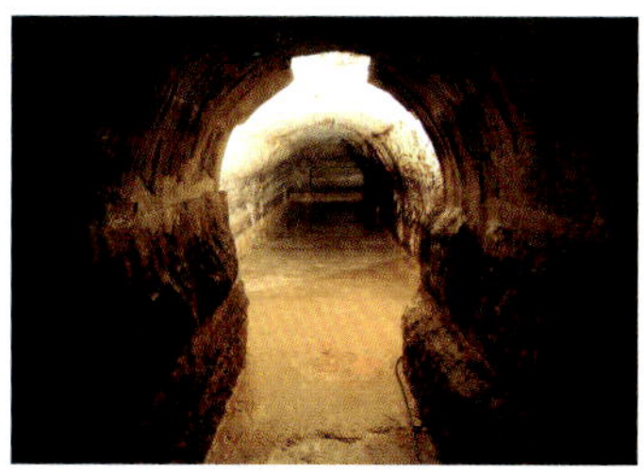

In addition to these five sites, the Museum manages the Roman Galleries of Rua da Prata, discovered underground in Lisbon in 1771. It is a cryptoportico (an underground passageway) built in the first century AD next to the port area of Felicitas Iulia Olisipo, as Lisbon was known in Roman times. It is only open to the public twice a year for reasons of preservation.

THE FIRST SETTLERS

Human occupation of the area started in the Palaeolithic, as the temporary settlements in the valley of the Alcântara stream date from around 10,000 BC. From the Neolithic onwards, human presence was concentrated mainly in the Volcanic Complex of Lisbon – which originated from the chain of volcanoes stretching from Mafra to the Range of Monsanto (Serra de Monsanto). During the Bronze Age, the existing social structure broke down and the large fortified settlements gave way to hierarchical communities with centralised power.

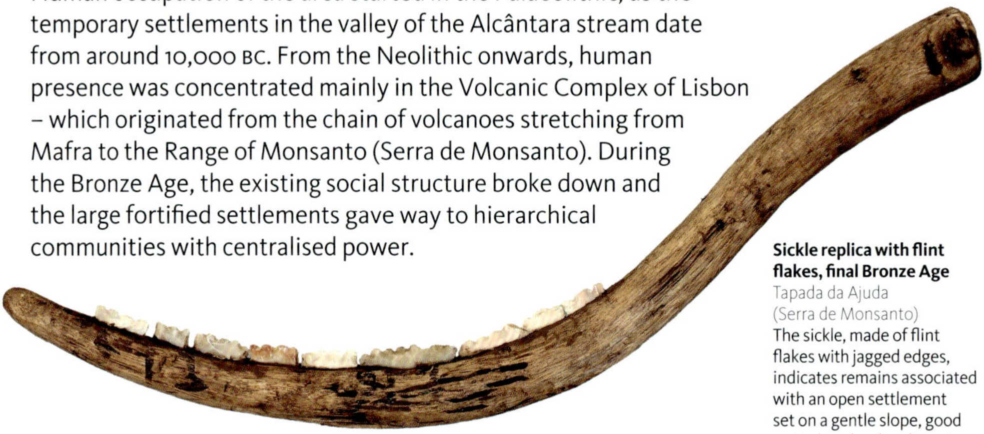

Sickle replica with flint flakes, final Bronze Age
Tapada da Ajuda (Serra de Monsanto)
The sickle, made of flint flakes with jagged edges, indicates remains associated with an open settlement set on a gentle slope, good agricultural soil and a water flow into the Tagus.

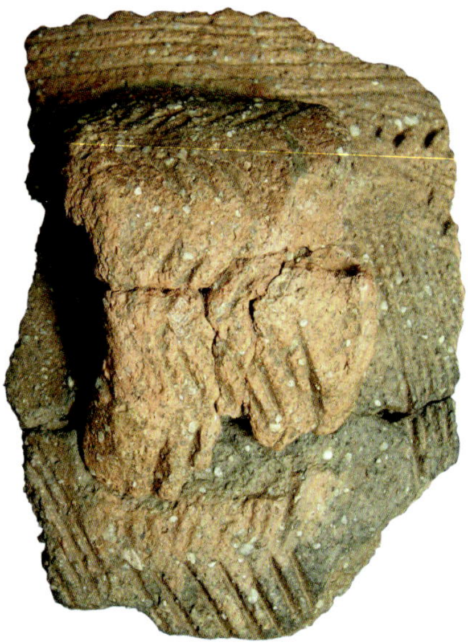

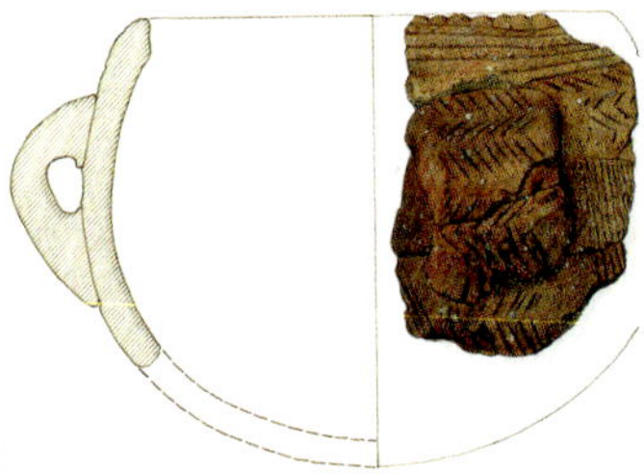

Pottery fragment, Neolithic
Vila Pouca settlement (Serra de Monsanto)
This fragment has a side handle and incised decoration.

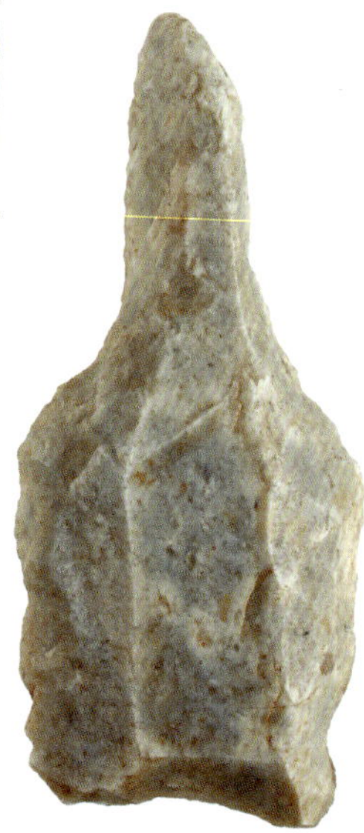

Flint awl, Neolithic
Vila Pouca settlement (Serra de Monsanto)
Trihedrons have multiple functions – this example was used for quartering game.

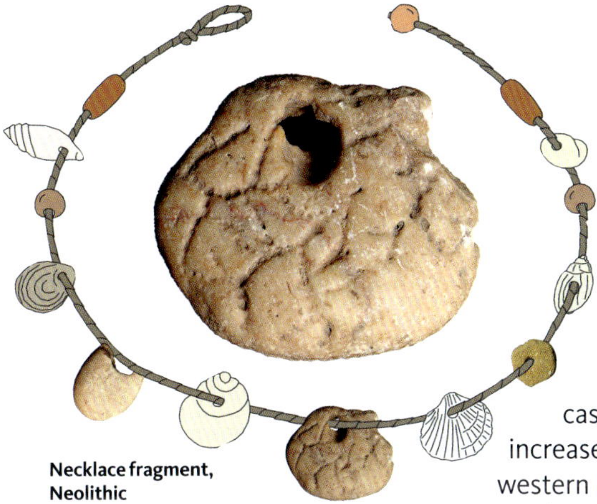

Necklace fragment, Neolithic
Vila Pouca settlement (Serra de Monsanto)
This small pebble formed part of a necklace. The upper half of the conical section is double drilled, for threading a cord.

The city of Lisbon began to develop from the Iron Age. The position of the Tagus estuary in the trade network established in the first millennium BC, along with the rich natural resources of the region, made it an important strategic hub targeted by traders from the eastern Mediterranean. In the eighth century BC the settlement located on the current castle hill and the waterfront developed through increased contact between local populations and the western Phoenicians.

Known after a certain point as Olisipo, *-ipo* meaning 'place on a high point' in the indigenous language of the southern peninsular, the settlement quickly prospered and became one of the largest in western Iberia during the Iron Age.

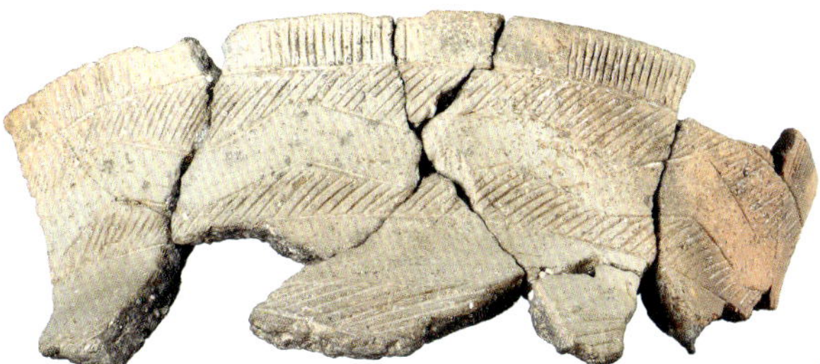

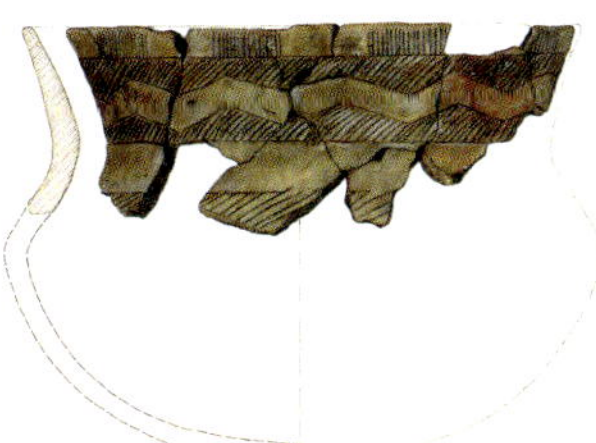

Pottery fragment, final Neolithic
Montes Claros settlement (Serra de Monsanto)

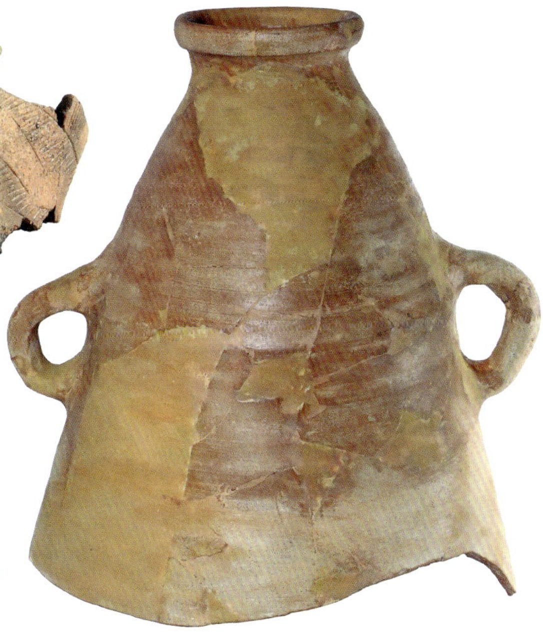

Amphora, mid-6th century BC (?)
Casa dos Bicos

THE ROMAN CITY OF FELICITAS IULIA OLISIPO

The Romans were present in Olisipo and the surrounding region from the late second century BC. The city enjoyed the privileged designation of *municipio romanorum* (Roman municipality), and during emperor Augustus' reign (27 BC to 14 AD) it was granted the name Felicitas Iulia Olisipo. When peace was declared throughout the empire in 16 BC, strong trade relations were established between its various regions.

The wealth of the city and the surrounding area was mainly generated by fishing, but also agricultural production. Thanks to its geographical position it became a prominent exporter of a variety of goods. In turn, new and diverse products flowed into the area. Olisipo quickly became the maritime capital of the Iberian Roman province of Lusitania, the western province of the Empire. The existence of several fish-processing factories in the riverside area bears witness to the vitality of this economic activity and other subsidiary industries, such as the production of ceramics to store the products.

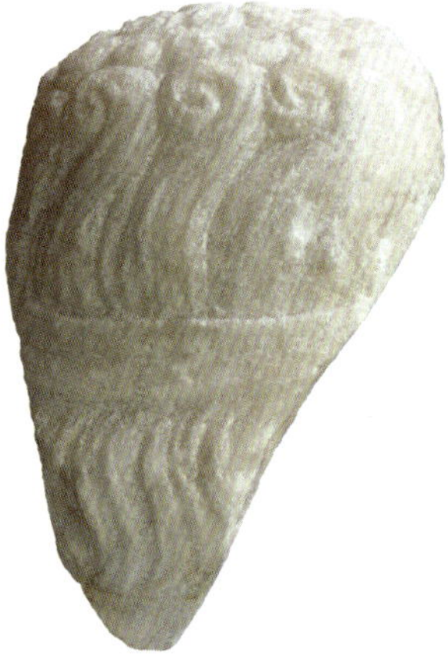

Statue head, mid-1st century AD
Archaeological excavation, 1964
This marble head fragment may represent the god Apollo or Dionysus. It displays a ribbon (*taenia*) which holds back part of the hair.

Statue of Silenus, mid-1st century AD
Collected 1798
A figure from Greco-Roman mythology, Silenus was the tutor and companion of the god Dionysus/Bacchus. This marble statue was originally in the upper part of the *proscaenium* (the wall separating the stage from the spectator area).

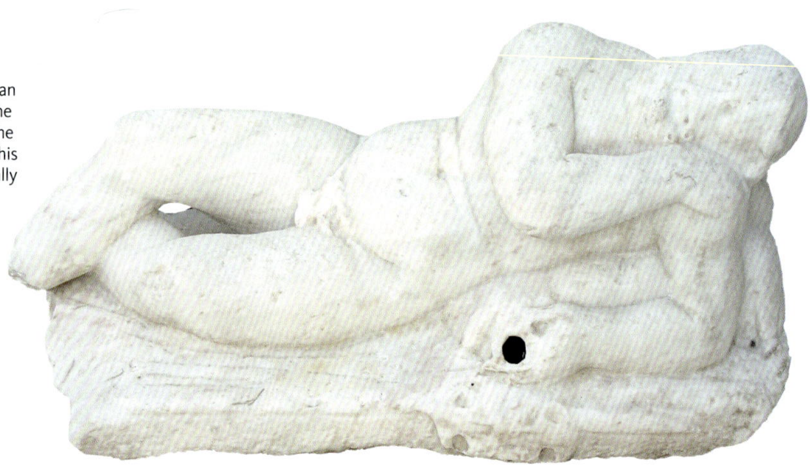

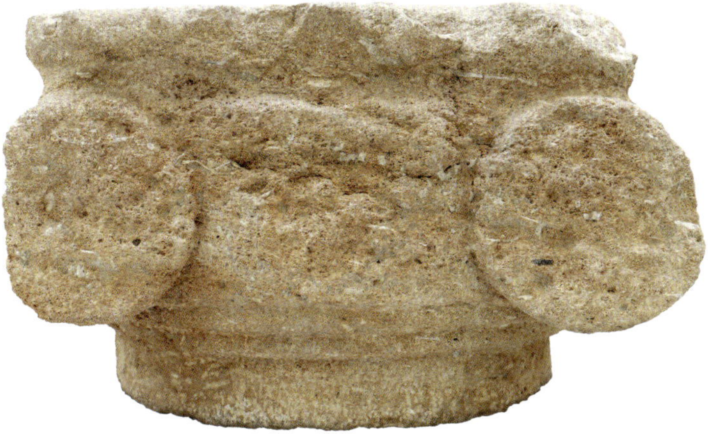

Ionic capital, early 1st century AD
Archaeological excavation, 1965/7
Only the inner part of the piece is preserved. It would once have been covered in plaster decorated with paint.

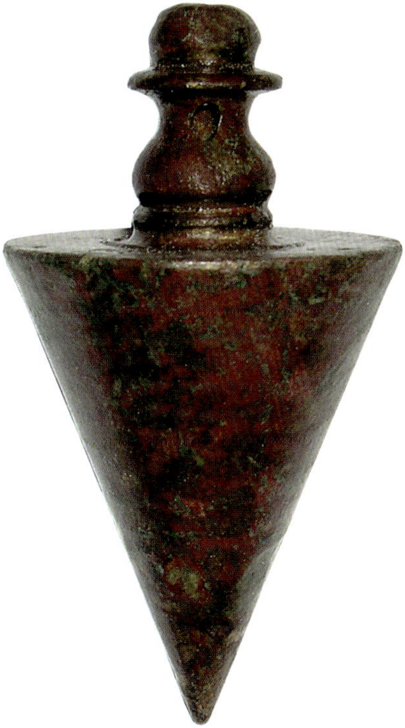

Plumb line, early 1st century AD
Archaeological excavation, 2005
This custom-made bronze plumb line may have been part of an apparatus called a *groma*, used to draw straight lines and right angles. It was used to make maps of cities and in the construction of buildings.

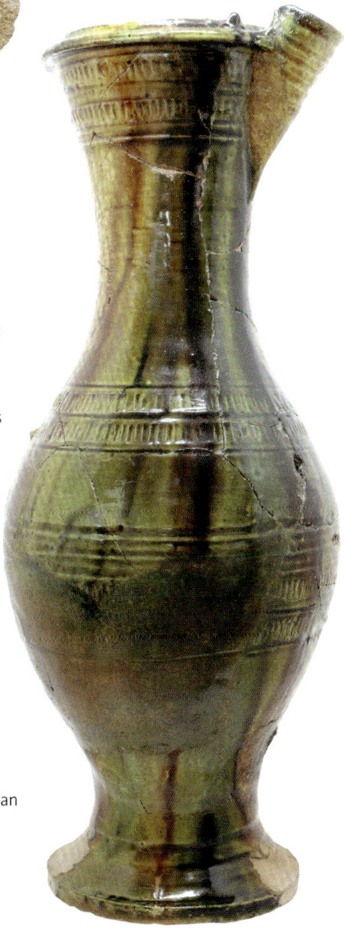

Pitcher, 14th century
Archaeological excavation, 2005
Found on the site of the Roman theatre, this clay pitcher of Parisian production is almost wholly preserved, decorated on the outside with a green and yellow glaze with rolled rectangular motifs imprinted on it.

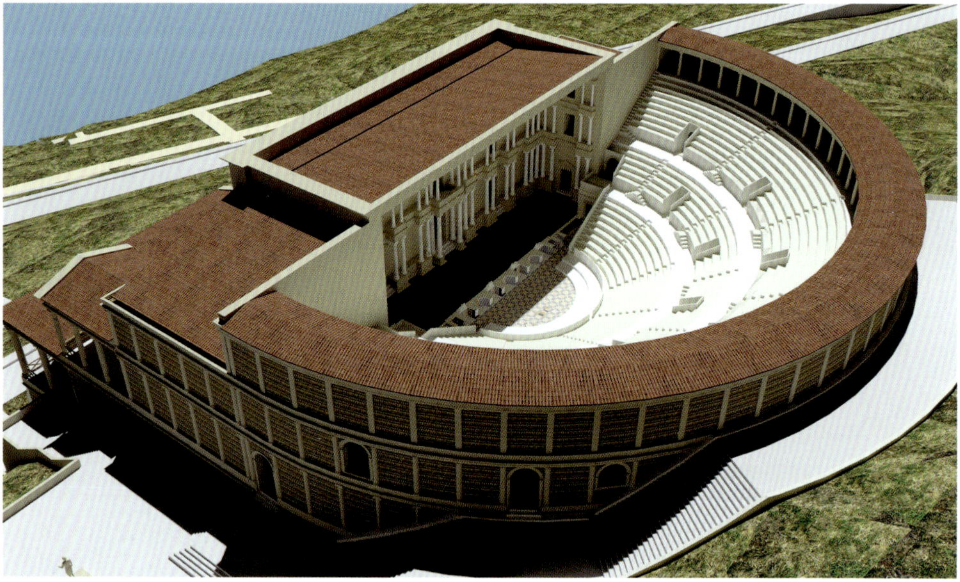

Roman theatre
Reconstruction Carlos Cabral Loureiro/Museum of Lisbon, 2015
Built in the early first century AD, the theatre was an important landmark in the city's landscape. The central part, the *orchestra*, and the lower steps of the seating area were cut into the rock, which was also used for architectural elements. An inscription on the wall of the *proscaenium* states that the theatre was renovated in AD 57.

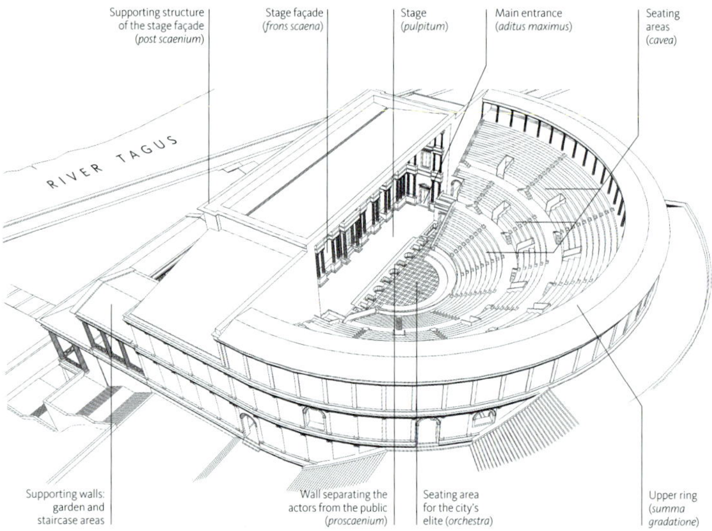

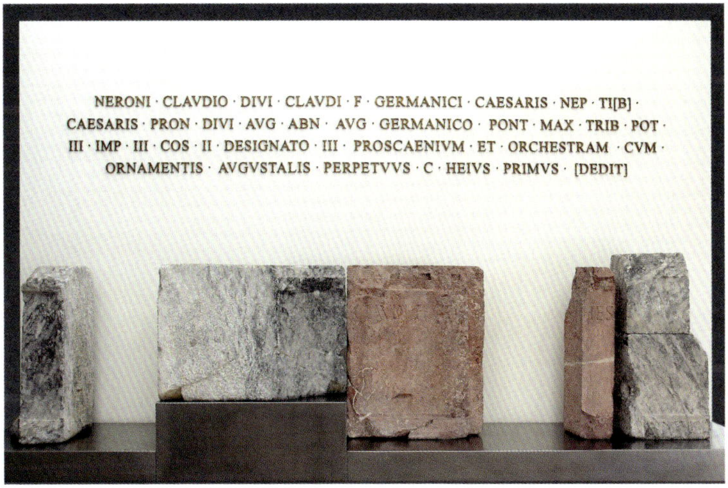

Structure of the *proscaenium*, AD 57
These stones formed part of the *frons pulpitum* (the façade in front of the spectators) of the *proscaenium*. The central part of the wall, which was almost 30 metres long, had several niches. An inscription written across the five central niches was dedicated to the emperor Nero.

Drawing of the remains of the Roman theatre discovered in 1798
This drawing shows what was visible at the time of the excavations, in a general plan and side elevation.

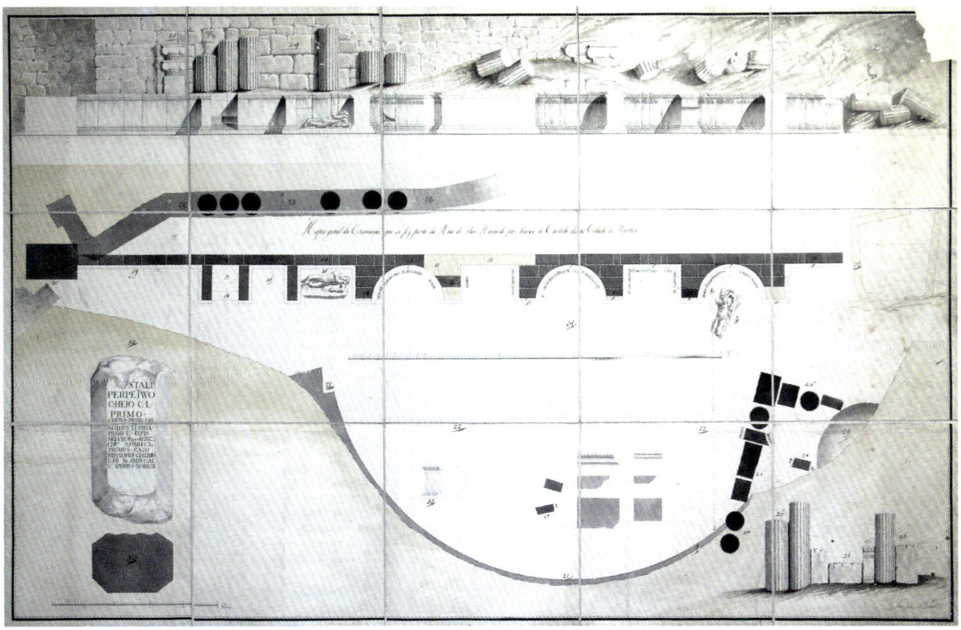

THE MEDIEVAL CITY

During the Islamic period, the city was known as al-Uxbuna. While maintaining the main routes from the Roman and Visigoth times, the city was progressively remodelled to encourage the organic grouping together of houses around winding roads. Three religions co-existed in the city under Moorish rule: Christianity, Islam and Judaism.

The ancient walls of the *alcáçova*, which is now the castle area, were rebuilt, and the administrative, political and military services were based there. The expansion of the walled perimeter led to the reconstruction of the Moorish (or Old) Wall, which circled the Medina, where the residential and commercial areas were located. It had markets (*souks*), mosques, baths and schools (*madrasas*).

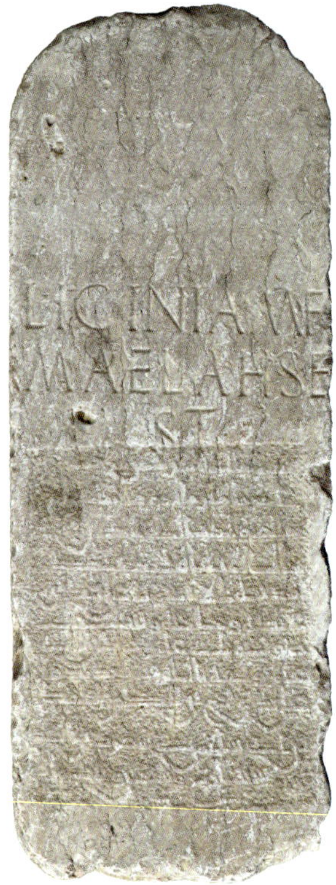

MUSLIM LISBON, 714–1147

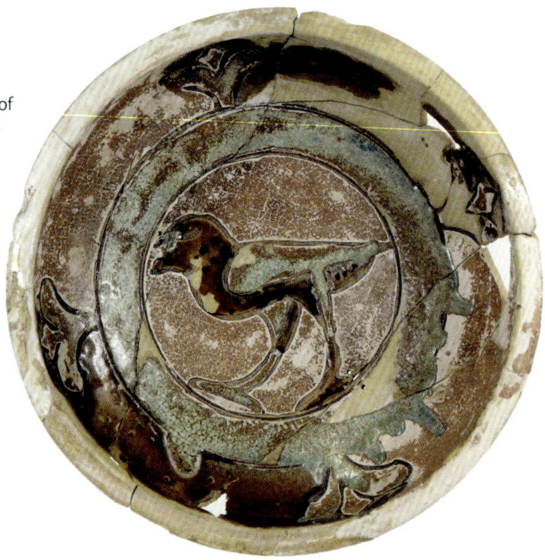

Glazed ware bowl, 11th/12th century
Rua das Pedras Negras
This imported piece, produced in the south of Al-Andalus, underlines the links between Lisbon and the southernmost parts of the Iberian Peninsula under Muslim rule, and the importance of the city's port in the medieval Islamic world.

Roman funerary stele with Arabic epigraph, 1st and 10th century AD
Castle of São Jorge
Beneath the Latin epitaph on this stele is a later Arabic inscription. The text describes the start of building works on Lisbon's *alcáçova* (castle) at the time of Hišām II and the sponsoring of the works by Almançor, Hišām's general.

Around the tenth century, two suburbs were formed near the main entrances of the city: next to Portas de Alfofa, to the west, the Muslim aristocracy created a residential suburb; and to the east, next to Portas do Sol, the Alfama suburb was linked to trade and riverside activities.

In 1147 Afonso Henriques, the first king of Portugal (r. 1143–85), conquered the Moors and reclaimed Lisbon. Christian rule led to economic, political and social changes. The king made specific laws for the Muslim and Jewish populations, who were each confined to their own living quarters. In 1496, by royal decree, those Muslims and Jews who wanted to live in the kingdom had to convert to Christianity. Those who didn't had to leave.

King Afonso III set up the Royal Chancellery in 1256, making it the capital of the kingdom which, together with the development of foreign trade, caused a growth in population and urban expansion.

Gravestone, 1398
Praça da Figueira
The headstone of the grave of Al-Abbas Ahmad, a member of the Muslim community of the city. The inscription names the deceased and the burial date (Monday 17 June 1398), and includes quotations from the Koran.

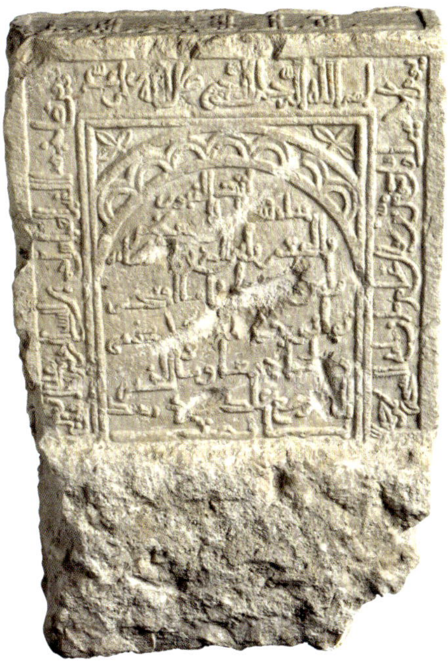

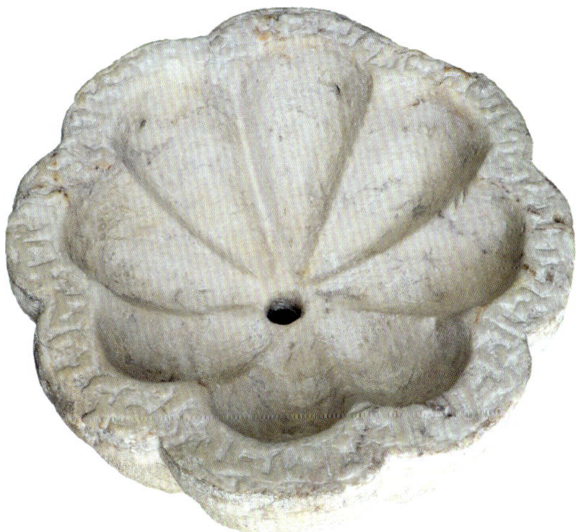

Ablutions font, 14th/15th century
Rua João do Outeiro
This font, which probably came from the old Mosque of Mouraria, would have been used for the ablutions that preceded prayer. Repeated along the edge of the stone is a Kufic inscription of the Arabic words 'Al-Mulk' – 'The Empire (of God)'. The hole at the bottom was drilled at a later date.

CHRISTIAN LISBON, 1147–1501

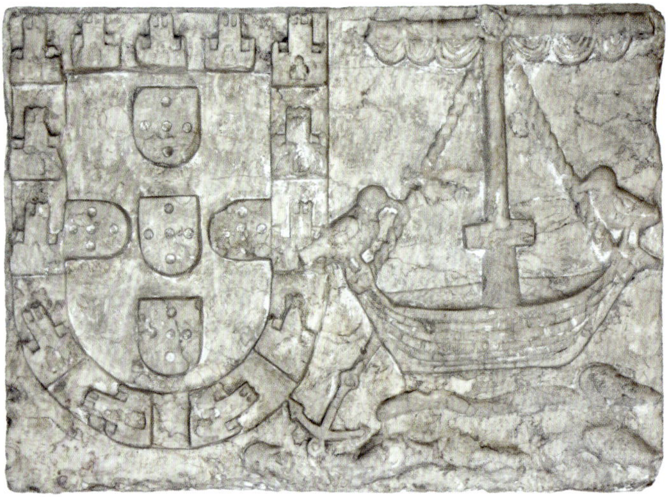

Coat of arms of the Kingdom of Portugal and the City of Lisbon, 1360
Fountain of Arroios
The coat of arms of the Kingdom of Portugal is made up of a shield with five escutcheons, alluding to the wounds of Christ, and castles representing fortresses taken from the Moors. The Lisbon coat of arms is inspired by the legend of St Vincent, patron saint of the city (see p. 22).

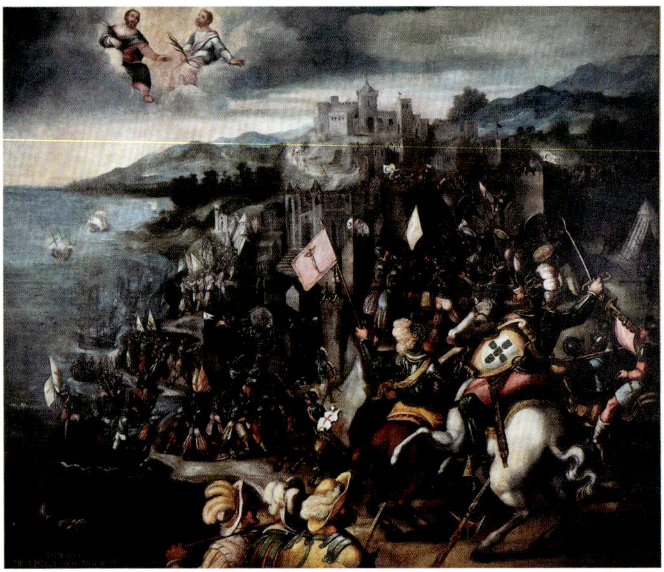

***The taking of Lisbon from the Moors*, mid-17th century**
Former Church of São Crispim and São Crispiniano
This painting depicts the ordeal of the holy martyrs Crispin and Crispinian, twin brothers who were beheaded in Soissons (France) during the persecution of the Christians in the early fourth century. Commemorated on 25 October, the date of the conquest of Lisbon by King Afonso Henriques, the brothers were adopted as the first patrons of the city.

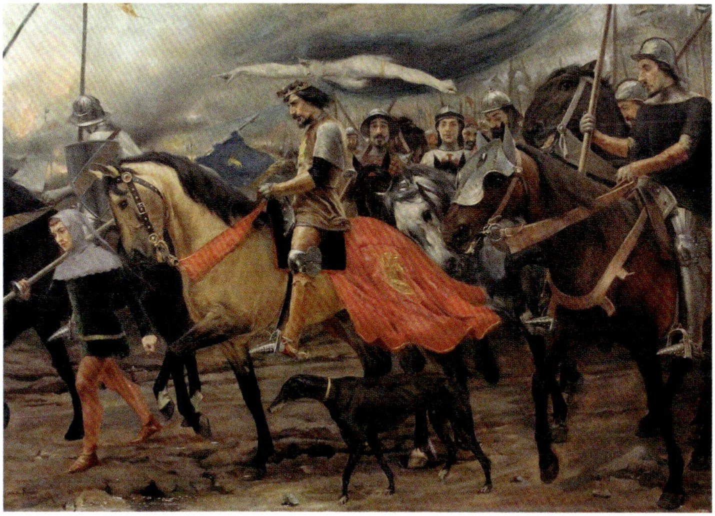

***Plague forcing the Castilians to lift the Siege of Lisbon*, 1901**
Constantino Fernandes
This painting alludes to an event that took place during the 1383–5 crisis. When King Fernando died without a male heir, King Juan of Castile, who was married to Fernando's daughter Beatriz, invaded Portugal under the pretence of unifying the two kingdoms, but the Plague forced him to return to Castile.

Scale model (hypothetical) of the Convento do Carmo in the 14th/15th century, 1989
Carlos Ribeiro (drawings)
Carlos Cabral Loureiro (construction)
Built on the hill overlooking the Rossio, the convent was founded in 1389 by Constable Nuno Álvares Pereira, in celebration of the victory over the Castilians (1385). Constable went on to become the richest man in the kingdom, receiving land that belonged to the nobles who took the side of Castile.

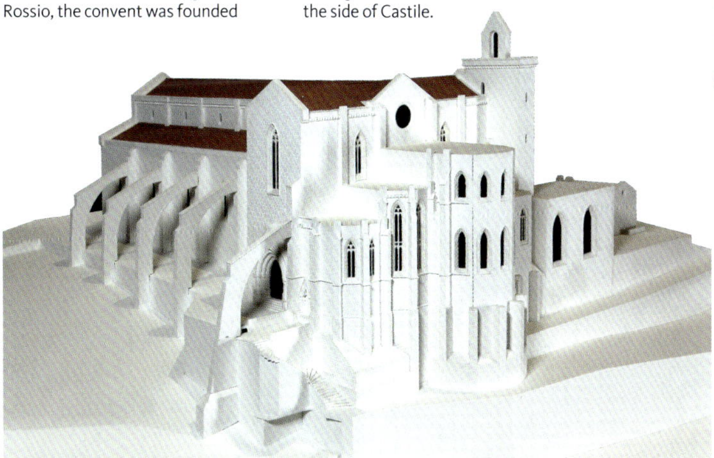

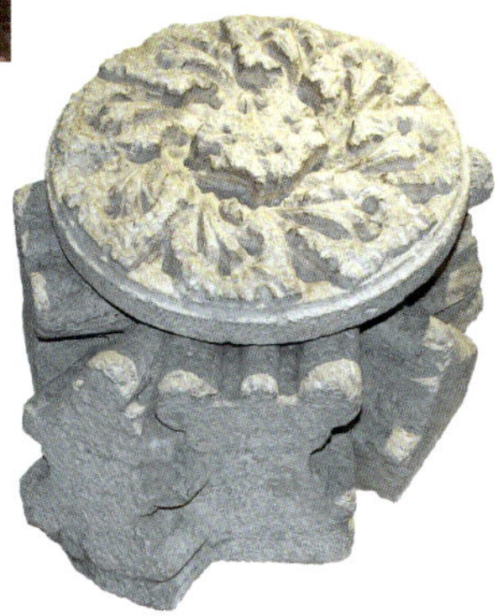

Arch stone, 15th century
Old Convent of Loios
Positioned at the highest point of a church's dome – to close it – this was the final piece to be placed. It was part of the Church of the Convent of Santo Elói, which belonged to the Congregation of the Seculares de São João Evangelista, commonly known as Loios, who took possession of the premises in 1442.

SAINT ANTHONY

Fernando de Bulhões (later known as St Anthony) was born in Lisbon around 1195 and studied with the canons of Lisbon Cathedral until he entered the Monastery of St Vincent as a novice. Two years later he was transferred to Santa Cruz Monastery in Coimbra. Whilst there, the remains of the bodies of five Franciscan monks who had been beheaded in Morocco were brought back to the city. This event led Fernando to change religious order (and his name) and to leave for Morocco to convert the people there. Illness prevented him from reaching Africa and a storm drove him to Italy, where he made his name as a skilled orator and preacher.
He died in 1231 and was made a saint less than a year later.

St Anthony's throne, 20th century

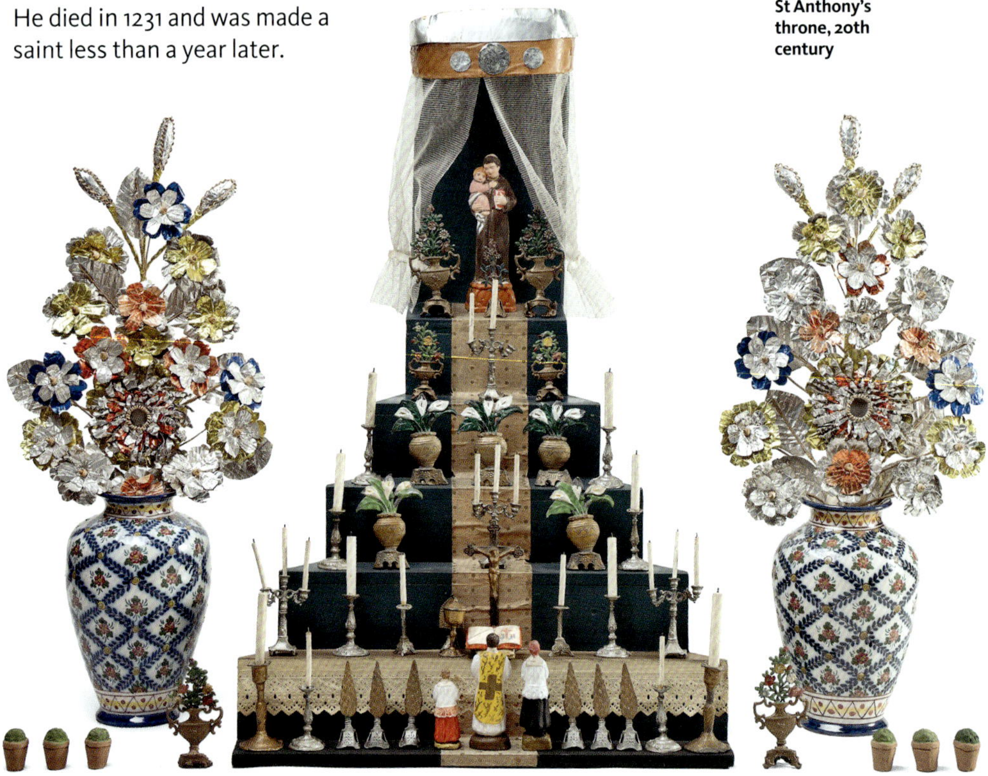

The Museum of Lisbon presents the saint's cultural importance both from a historical and religious viewpoint, as well as acknowledging his social and anthropological significance. This is why the museum places such emphasis on the popular facet of the saint and all the festivities held in the city in June.

St Anthony is traditionally depicted in the Franciscan habit – a brown tunic with a cord at his waist and sandals on his feet. The original symbol representing the saint was the Bible. Yet from the sixteenth century onwards it is the figure of the baby Jesus himself who is most popularly associated with the saint.

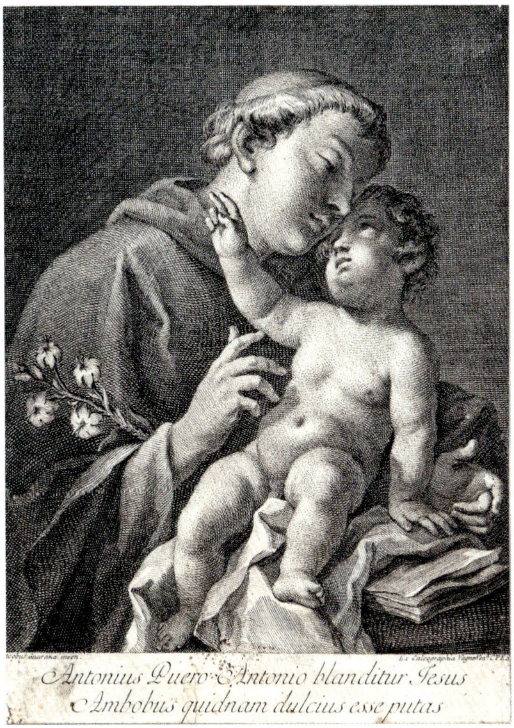

St Anthony with the baby Jesus, 18th century
Jacob Guarana

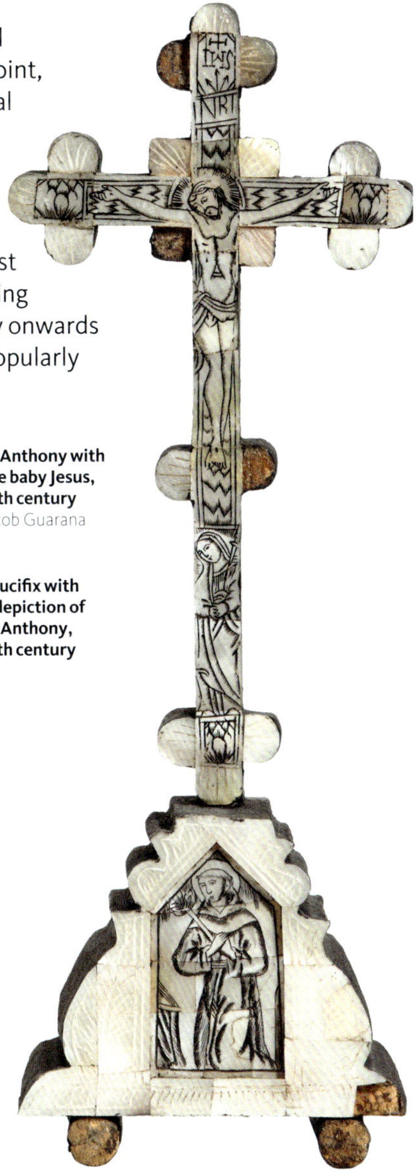

Crucifix with a depiction of St Anthony, 17th century

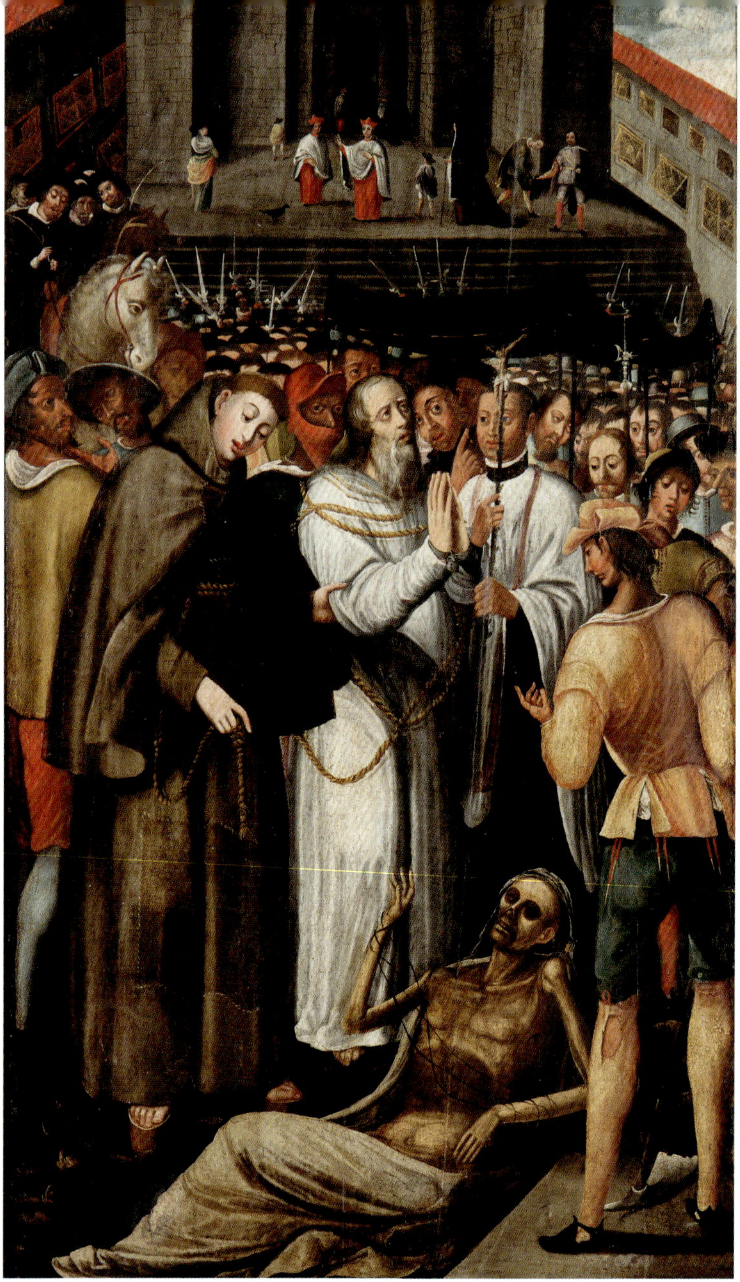

St Anthony freeing his father from the gallows, 16th century

St Anthony, 16th century

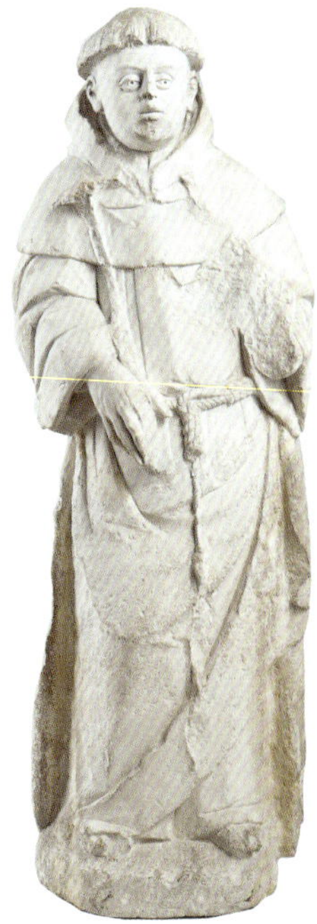

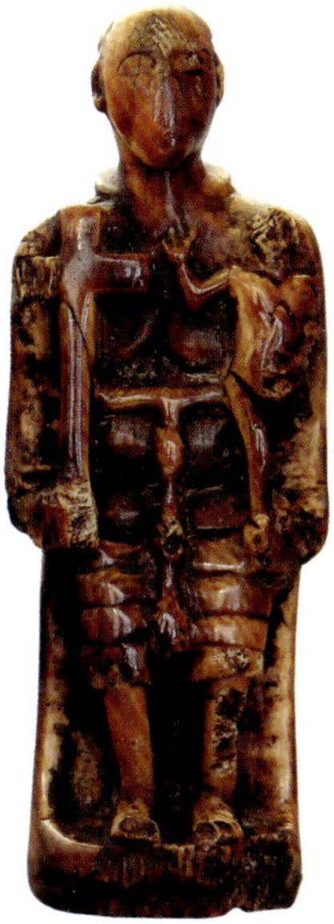

Toni Malau (or St Anthony of Good Fortune), 17th century
This small ivory sculpture reveals a little-known facet of the cult of St Anthony, whose image with the baby Jesus on his lap is common in many cultures around the world. Originating in the ancient Kingdom of Kongo, it illustrates the fusion of African culture and Christianity introduced by Europeans. Used as a kind of amulet, the statue served to protect its owner from enemies, to intercede on their behalf in times of trouble or to rescue ships during storms.

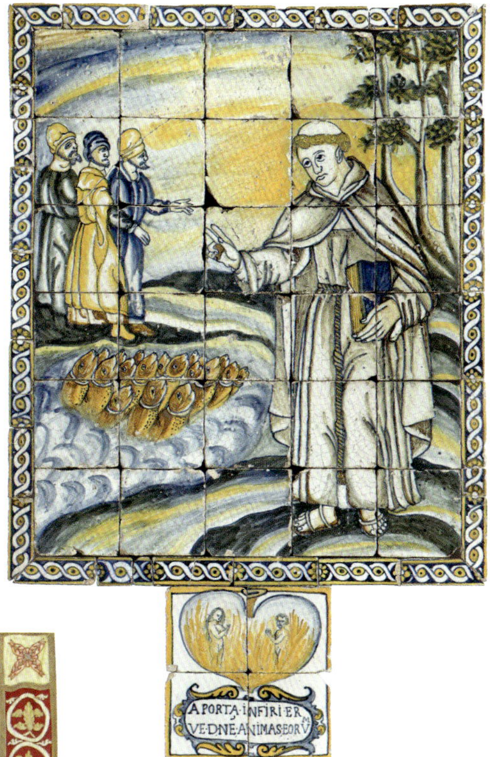

Sermon of St Anthony to the fish, 17th century
This tile panel was originally situated on the steps of a street in the Jogo da Pela area of Lisbon.

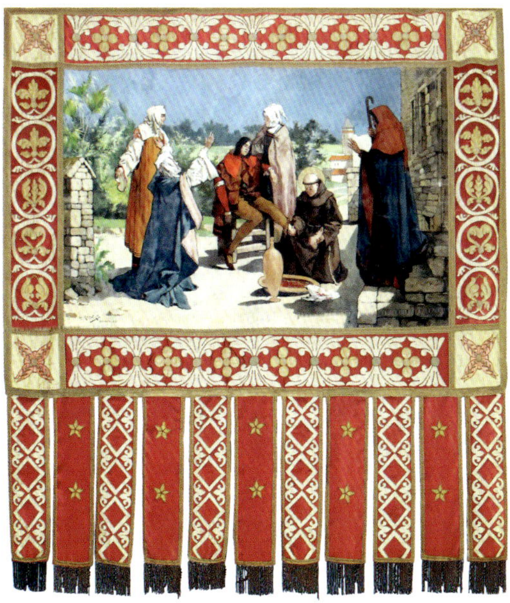

***The miracle of the reattached foot*, 1895**
Jos Ratinck (painting)
D. Vansina (embroidery)
Part of a series of ten, this banner was produced in Antwerp to commemorate the seventh centenary of the birth of St Anthony. It alludes to the story of a young boy who cut off his own foot in despair at having harmed his mother; the saint miraculously reattached the foot to the boy's leg.

CAPITAL CITY OF A MARITIME EMPIRE

King João II (r. 1481–95) turned navigational exploration into a state enterprise, making Lisbon the main base of overseas expansion, beginning in 1415 with the conquest of Ceuta on the north coast of Africa. The population growth in the early fifteenth century led to the construction of the new town, Olival ao Carmo, from 1502, the first trial of a new city with a planned layout. The city's needs grew as Atlantic expansion and overseas trade increased.

The resulting area of landfill sites along the river was limited on the east side by Alfândega Nova (New Customs). To the west were the shipyards and the buildings of the House of India, next to which the king built the Palace of Ribeira (1498–1503). The new square, Terreiro do Paço (Palace Square), became the city's administrative, commercial and financial centre. The city started to grow around the riverbank, between the convent of Madredeus in Xabregas, to the east, and the monastery of Jerónimos in Belém, to the west.

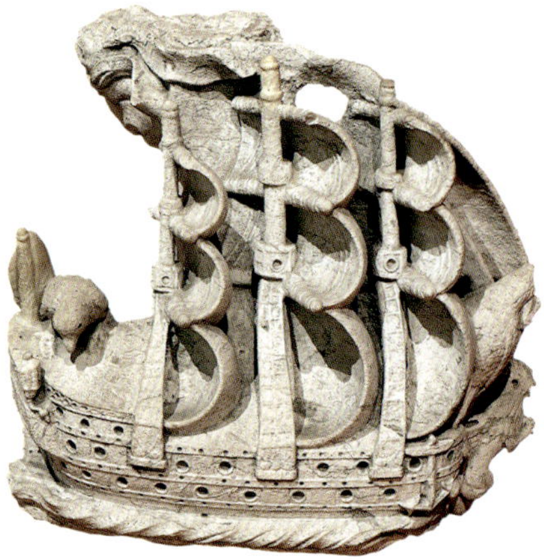

Coat of arms of the city, mid-/late 16th century
Rua dos Arameiros
According to legend, the body of St Vincent was brought ashore in Cabo de São Vicente, and a shrine erected at his grave, which was always guarded by ravens. When the first Portuguese king, Afonso Henriques, had the body of the saint exhumed in 1173 and brought by ship to Lisbon, the ravens accompanied the boat. This transfer of the relics is depicted on the Lisbon coat of arms.

Mudejar tile panels with Renaissance decoration, early/mid-16th century
Seville production
Wall tiles from the first half of the sixteenth century show the strong influence of Mudejar decorative tradition.

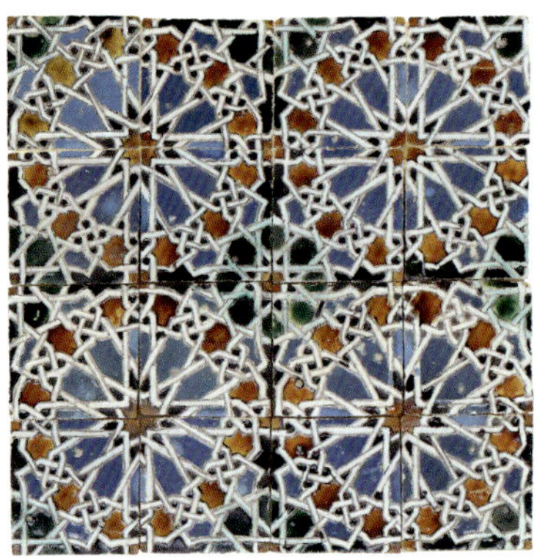

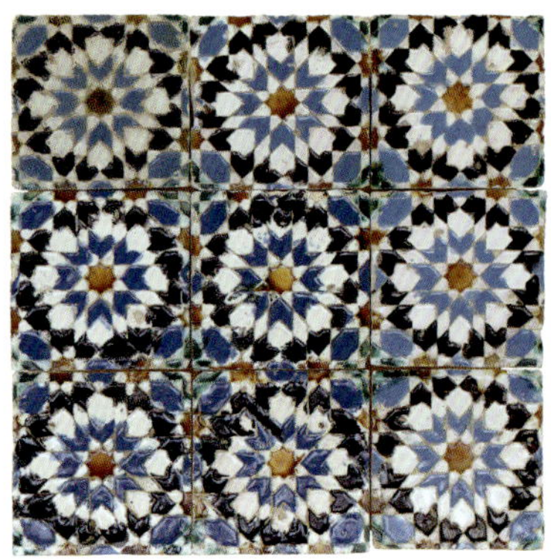

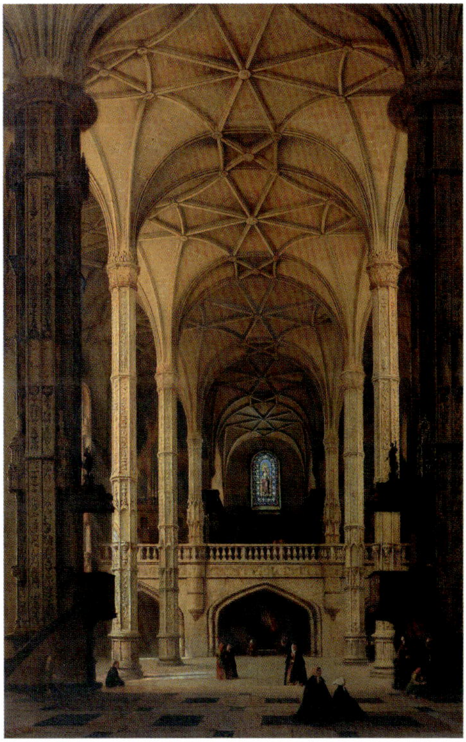

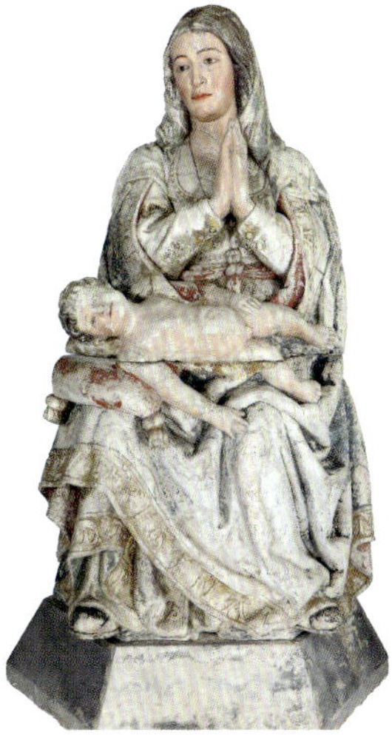

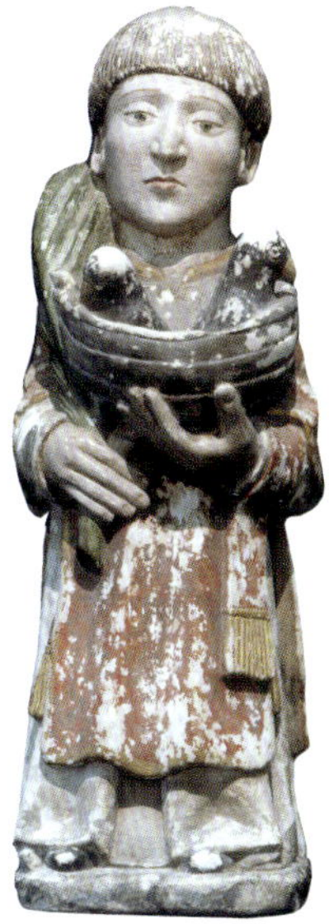

St Vincent the Martyr, 15th century

Virgin and Child, 16th century
Church of St Lawrence (today part of Rosa Palace)
Many Lisboners felt a great affection for this statue, known as Our Lady of Childbirth. It probably dates from after 1531, when the church was partially destroyed by an earthquake.

***Jerónimos Monastery*, mid-/late 19th century**
Tony de Bergue
The Monastery of Santa Maria de Belém, better known as Jerónimos Monastery, was commissioned by King Manuel I (r. 1495–1521). Designed as a monastery and royal pantheon, it was the main royal building project of the time (started around 1501) and was donated to the friars of the Order of St Jerome.

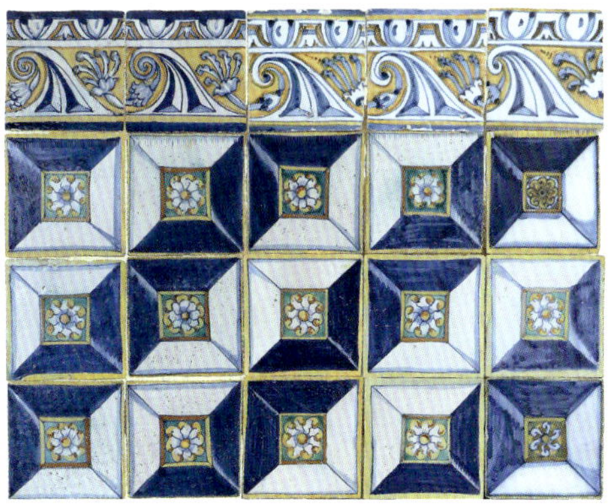

'Carpet' tile panel decorated in 'diamond point' with a 'wolf tooth' border, early 17th century
Local production (Lisbon?)
'Carpet' tiles are so called because of the textile effect they create with their geometric motifs.

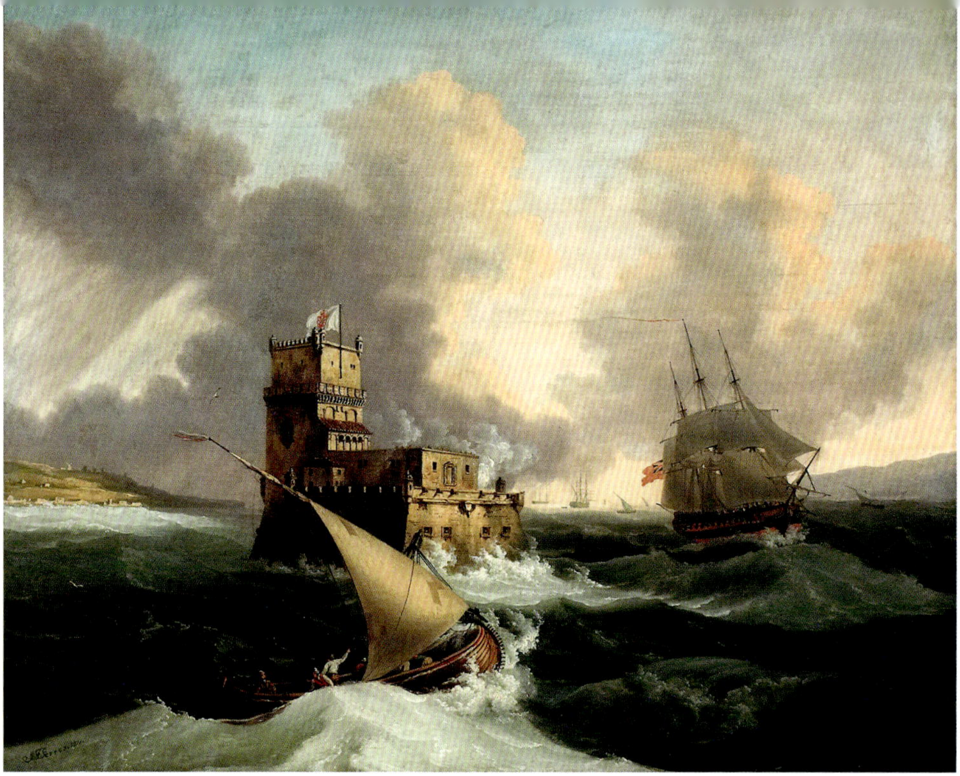

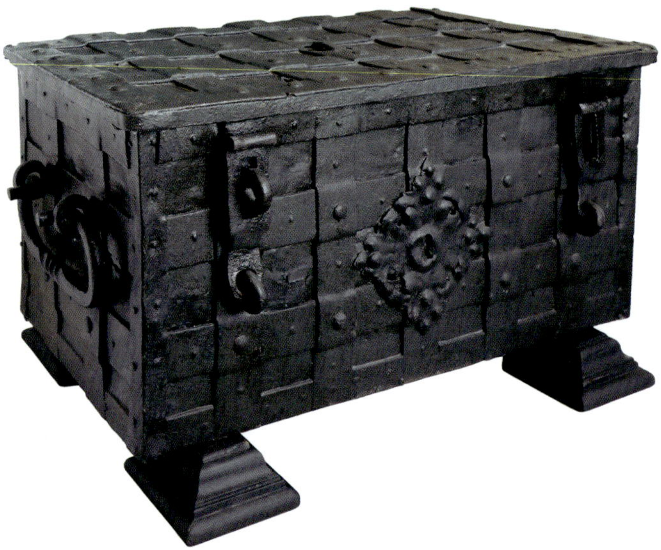

***Tower of Belém*, 1811**
John Thomas Serres
As part of a larger project to defend the River Tagus estuary, the Tower of São Vicente (also known as the Tower of Belém), was built in 1515–19 facing the Tower of São Sebastião da Caparica on the opposite side of the river.

Chest, 16th century
Portuguese (?)
Paços do Concelho de Lisboa (Lisbon City Hall)
Chests such as these were common in the sixteenth century among noblemen travelling by ship, due to their versatility and the ease with which they could be moved around.

FROM SPANISH RULE TO THE SPLENDOUR OF THE BAROQUE

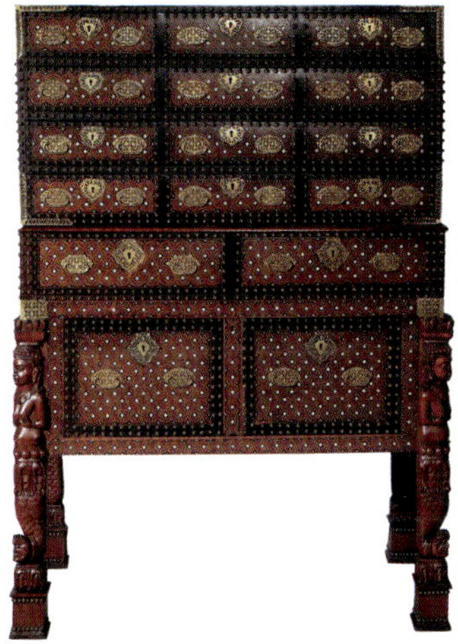

During the Philippine dynasty (1580–1640), Lisbon differed little in urban terms from the early-sixteenth-century city. The redesign of Paço da Ribeira (Ribeira Palace) was one of the first concerns of King Philip I (r. 1580–98). The new project enlarged the façade facing the square and included the construction of a tower to the south. The architect was Felipe Terzi (1520–1597) and the tower soon became the emblem of Lisbon.

With the recovery of national independence in 1640, the country endured a period of austerity. Except for the building of convents and royal works to fortify the city, urban renewal was postponed until the first half of the eighteenth century.

During the reign of King João V (r. 1706–50), many riches, including large amounts of gold and diamonds, were brought from Brazil to Lisbon. The king commissioned monumental buildings, designed mostly by foreign architects. A policy of spatial planning was established along the riverside, creating several quays, and the king also backed the construction of the future Royal Factory of Silks, which opened in 1741. The most ambitious project was the Águas Livres (Free Waters) Aqueduct and the network of public fountains linked to it, which resulted in the city having a modern and reliable water supply system.

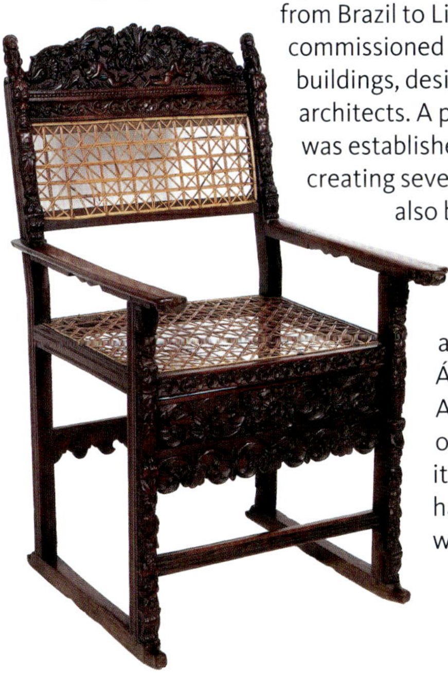

Cabinet on stand (contador), 17th century (?)
Indo-Portuguese
'Contador' is the Portuguese term for a cabinet. They were produced by Indian craftsmen using precious woods, meticulous inlays and intricate decoration.

Chair with arm-rests, 17th century
Indo-Portuguese
This piece illustrates the dual influence of European and Goan (India) aesthetics. Among the carved motifs are the naginis, Hindu mythological figures.

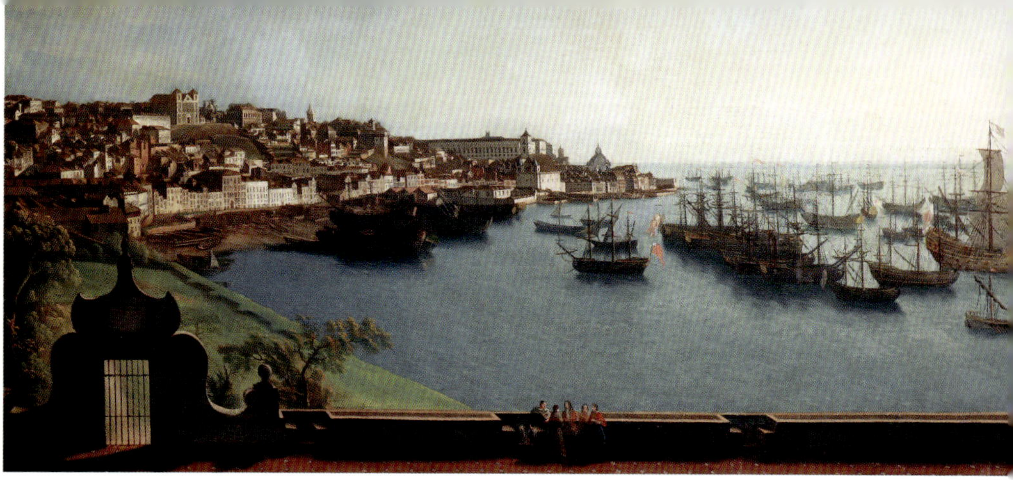

***Lisbon seen from the Palace of the Marquis of Abrantes*, early/mid-18th century**
This panorama of riverside Lisbon shows the area of the old port, in the small bay facing Boavista Street.

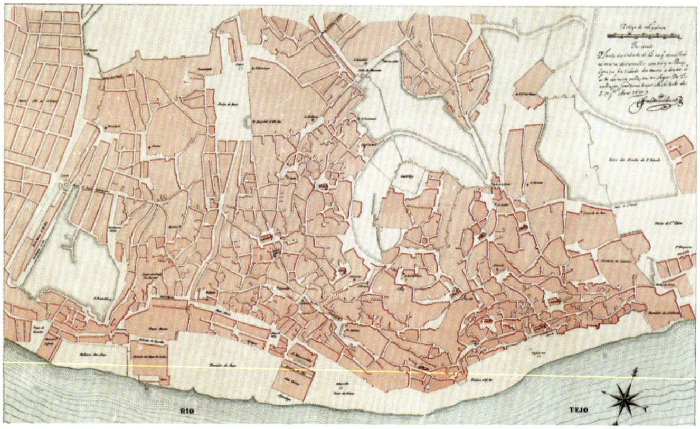

Plan of the City of Lisbon in 1650, 1850
Copy of original
by João Nunes Tinoco
This map of Lisbon is the oldest known plan of the city. It was drawn up in 1650, when King João IV was looking into ways to defend the city in the event of another Spanish invasion.

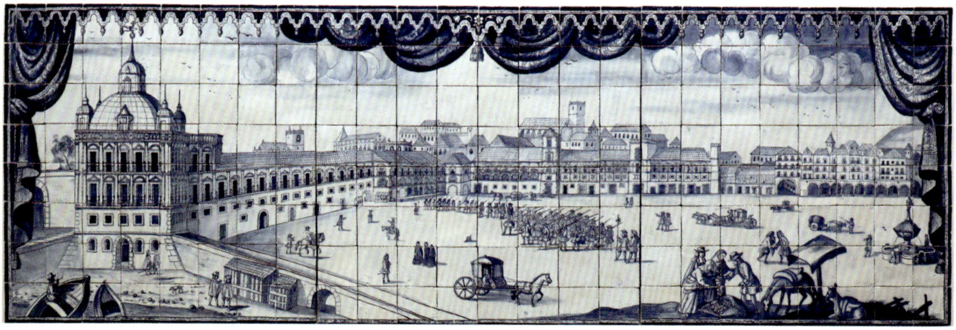

OPPOSITE BOTTOM:

Terreiro do Paço tile panel, early 18th century

Master P.M.P. (attributed)
Local production (Lisbon)

Terreiro do Paço was the political, civic and social centre of Lisbon between the 16th and 20th centuries. Ribeira Royal Palace is shown on the left, with a military parade and saleswomen selling their products.

THIS PAGE BELOW:

All Saints' Royal Hospital, early 18th century

Master P.M.P. (attributed)
Local production (Lisbon)

Rossio, home to the All Saints' Royal Hospital, destroyed by the 1755 earthquake, was the second most important square in Lisbon. In the foreground of this panel, several people are shown trading goods; on the left is the Neptune Fountain.

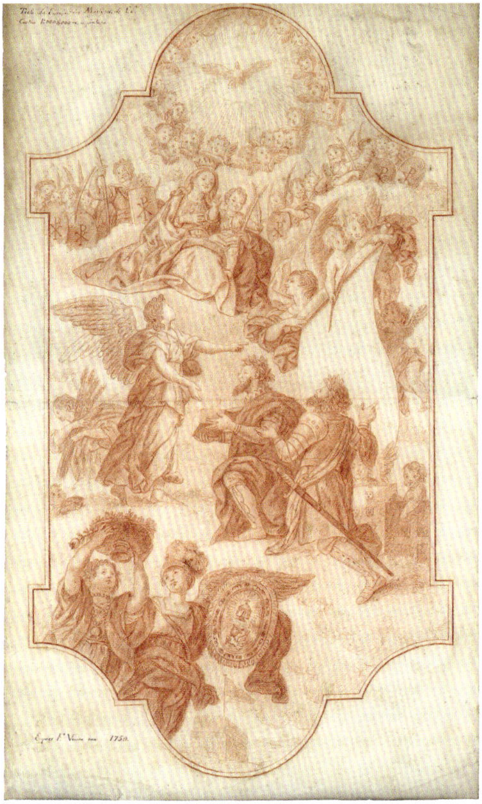

Preparatory drawing for the ceiling of the Church of the Martyrs, 1750

Francisco Vieira de Matos (Vieira Lusitano)

King Afonso Henriques laid the first stone of the church building on 21 November 1147, to pay tribute to the crusaders who died in the conquest of Lisbon. King João V ordered the church to be rebuilt after a fire destroyed it in 1746, commissioning Vieira Lusitano to decorate the ceiling. This work was destroyed by the 1755 earthquake and is known only through drawings.

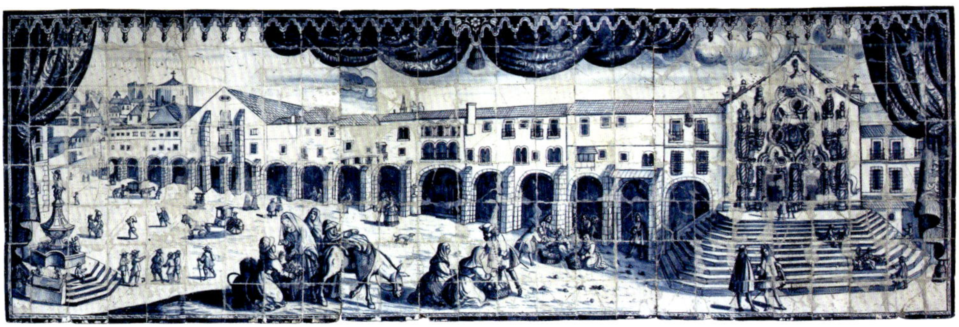

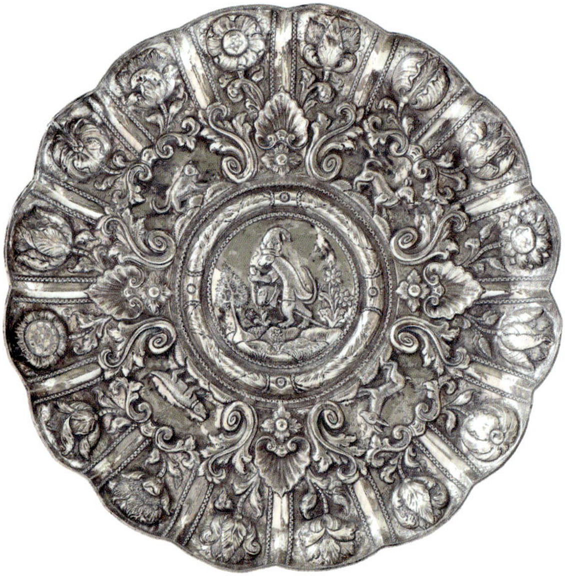

Silver salver, late 17th/early 18th century
An excellent example of a Baroque salver, this high-quality chiselled piece includes many elements of the broad repertoire of Lisbon's goldsmiths in the reign of King João V.

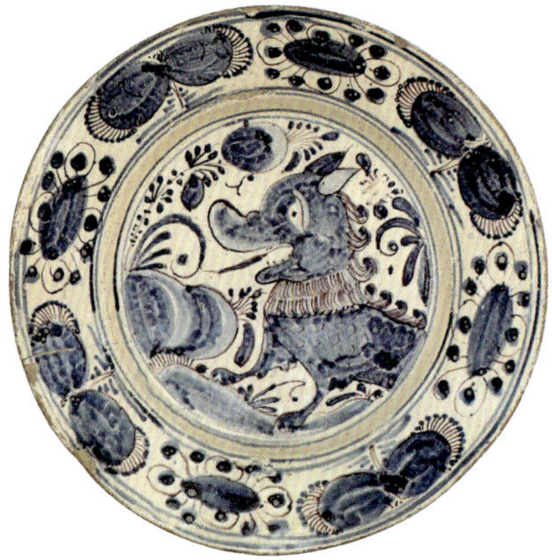

'Spider' dish, 1660–1700
Local production (Lisbon)
'Spider' ceramics reproduce in a basic style elements represented in Chinese porcelain. This lower-quality pottery (in artistic terms) would have been used by the less affluent classes. The leaf designs on the border have 'spider leg' additions, hence their name.

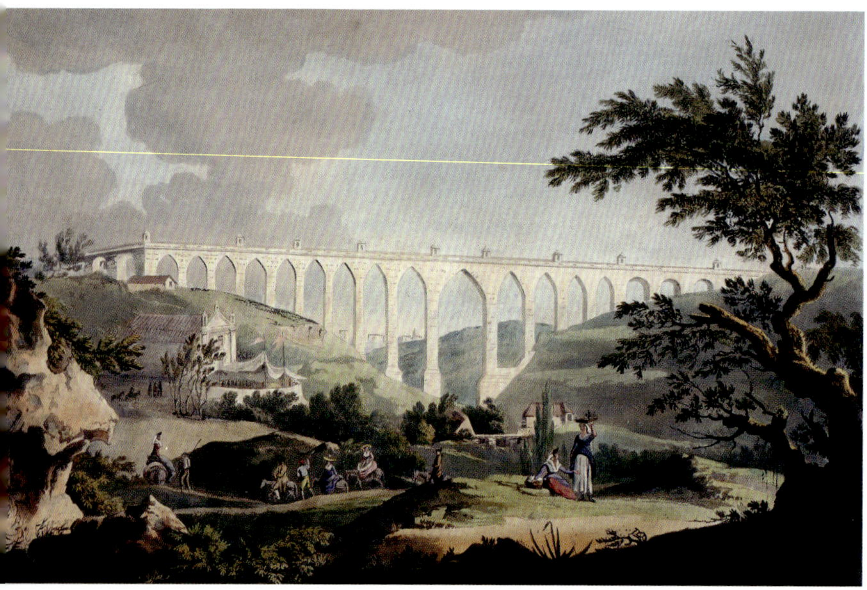

***A S.W. view of the grand aqueduct over the valley of Alcântara near Lisbon*, 1792**
Alexandre Jean Noel (drawing)
John Wells (engraving)
The section of arcades over the Alcântara valley is the most monumental section of the aqueduct. It is 941 metres long, and composed of 35 arches.

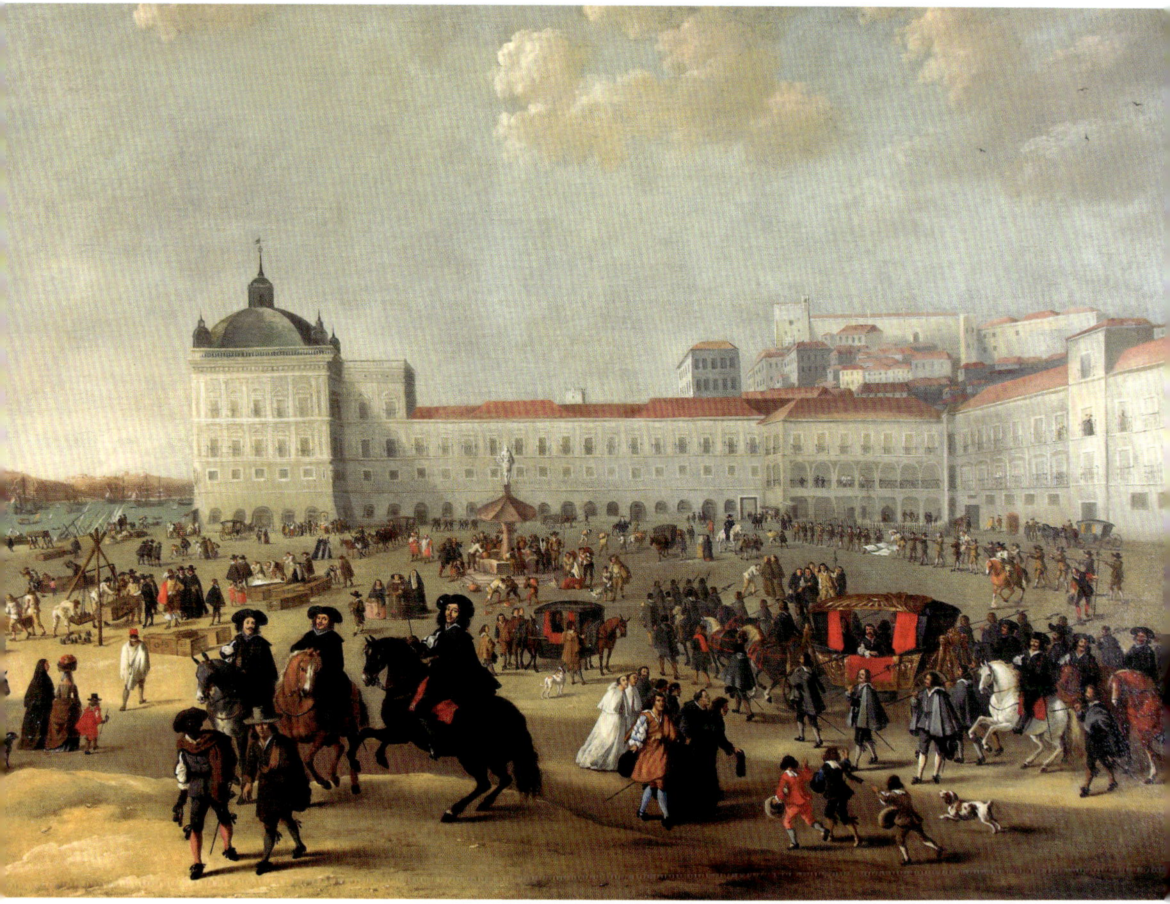

***Terreiro do Paço in the 17th century*, 1662**
Dirk Stoop

This is one of the most important views painted of Terreiro do Paço. It was identified as a possible representation of the arrival in Lisbon of Francisco de Mello e Torres, the 'extraordinary ambassador' of Portugal in London, after he had negotiated the Treaty of Whitehall (23 June 1661) and the marriage of Catherine of Braganza to Charles II of England. The view here highlights the multifunctional character of the square, where people of all social classes crossed paths.

THE EARTHQUAKE OF 1755

What crime, what error did these children,
Crushed and bloody on their mothers' breasts, commit?
Did Lisbon, which is no more, have more vices
Than London and Paris immersed in their pleasures?
Lisbon is destroyed, and they dance in Paris.

VOLTAIRE, 'Poem on the Lisbon Disaster', 1755

On 1 November 1755, at around 9.40am, Lisbon was hit by an earthquake. In the central part of the city, it is estimated that the magnitude was 9 on the Richter scale. There followed a tsunami and a fire that lasted six days. These caused the destruction of the neighbourhoods of the downtown area (Baixa) and the death of an estimated 10,000 to 30, 000 people, of whom only eight were of the nobility due to the fact that the king and court had not yet returned to Lisbon after the summer. The population of Lisbon was around 250,000 before the earthquake; by 1756, that number had dropped to approximately 165,000, not only due to the numbers who had lost their lives but also because many survivors had left the city.

OPPOSITE PAGE:
***St Nicholas' Church*, 1757**
Jacques Philippe Le Bas, Miguel Tibério Pedegache

***Opera House*, 1757**
Jacques Philippe Le Bas, Miguel Tibério Pedegache

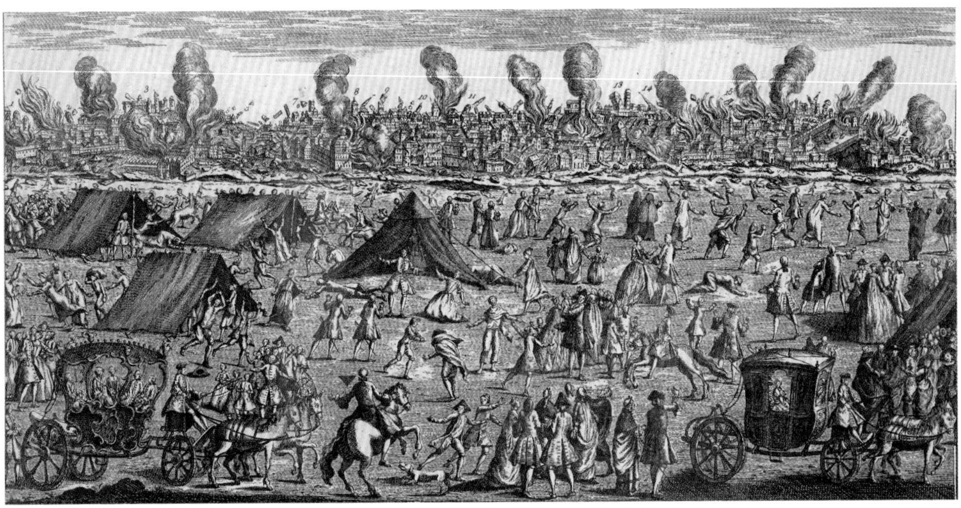

***Sad image of the effects caused by the earthquake*, mid-/late 18th century**

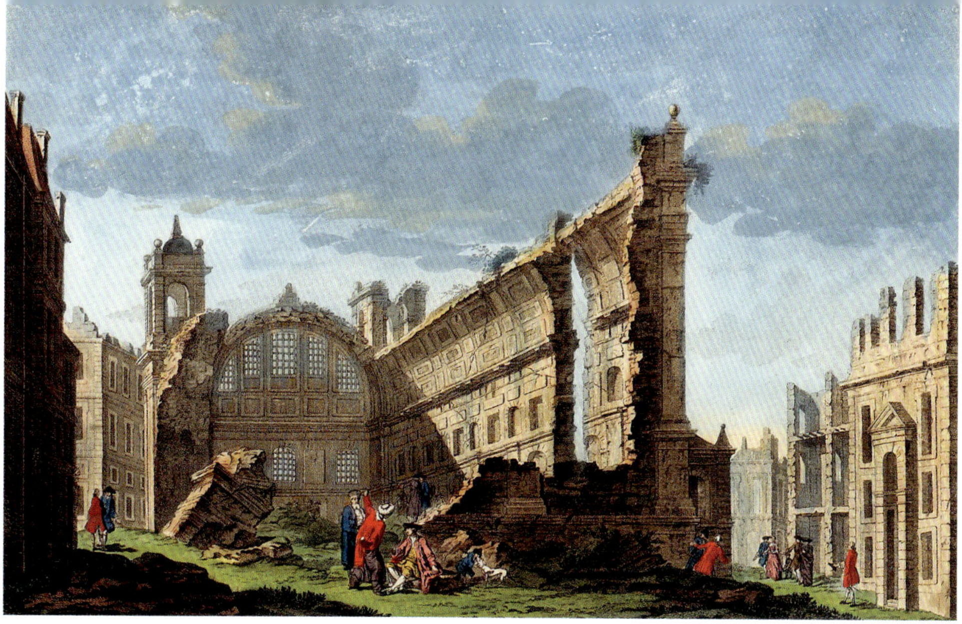

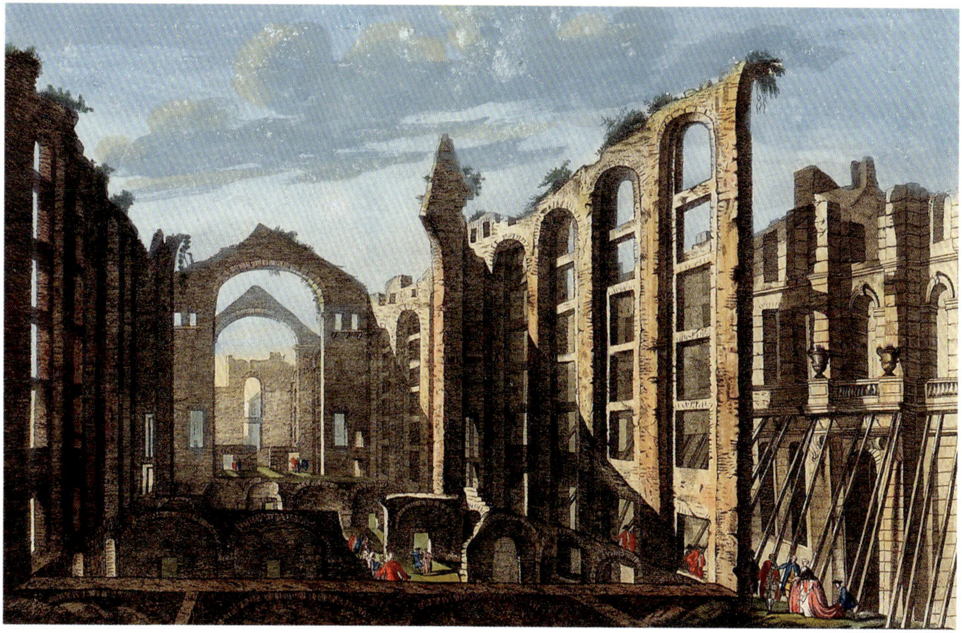

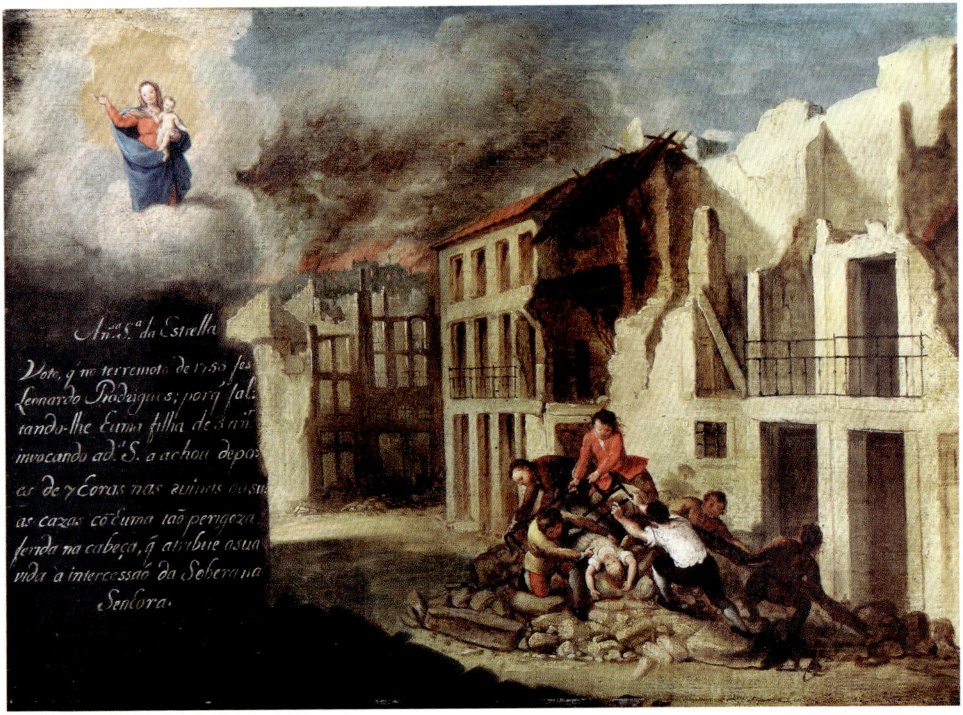

ABOVE: ***Ex-voto to Our Lady of Estrela*, mid-/late 18th century**
The painting depicts a child being rescued from the rubble caused by the earthquake, the scene witnessed by Our Lady of Estrela. The painting was ordered by Leonardo Rodrigues, whose daughter, after being buried for seven hours, was miraculously saved thanks to the intercession of the Virgin.

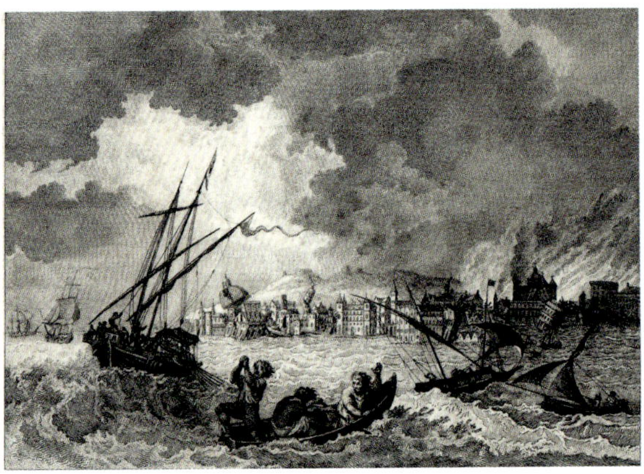

LEFT: ***Lisbon Earthquake in the year 1755*, 1781–1816**
Reinier Vinkeres, François Bohn
Soon after the earthquake, some people attempted to escape by boat and faced the waves of the tsunami on the river. In a small boat, a person is shown praying, pleading for divine intervention in the face of certain death.

Glazed Baroque tile, mid-18th century
Bartolomeu Antunes (attributed)
Many factors made Lisbon vulnerable to fires: scarcity of water, the choice of building materials, the city's urban layout – with its narrow, winding streets – and the lack of effective means to combat fire. After the disaster there was a strong increase in devotion to São Marçal (St Martial), protector against fire, who is depicted here.

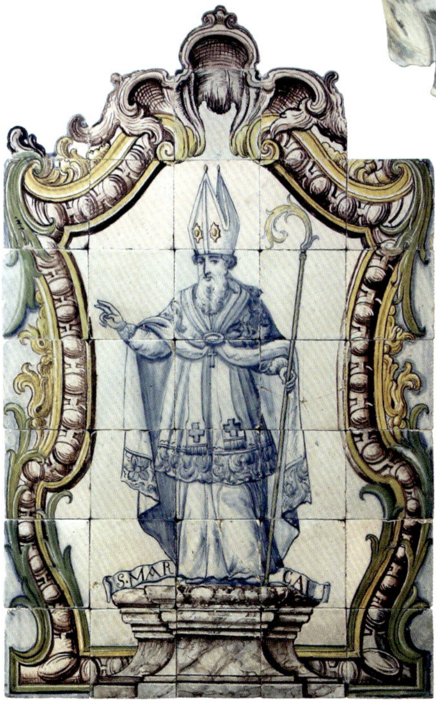

Vessel with lid, early 18th century
China (Qing dynasty)
The damage to this porcelain vessel was sustained at the moment the earthquake struck and in the fire that followed. It shows part of the melted pulp caused by the high temperatures of the fire.

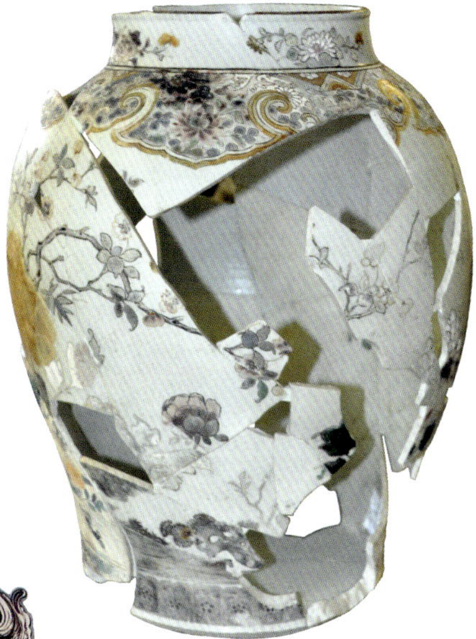

Walking stick handle
Walking sticks demonstrated a certain social prestige. This handle has three rows of diamonds, a cameo relief in ivory and is mounted with a female figure in classical style. It was found in a house that had been destroyed by the earthquake.

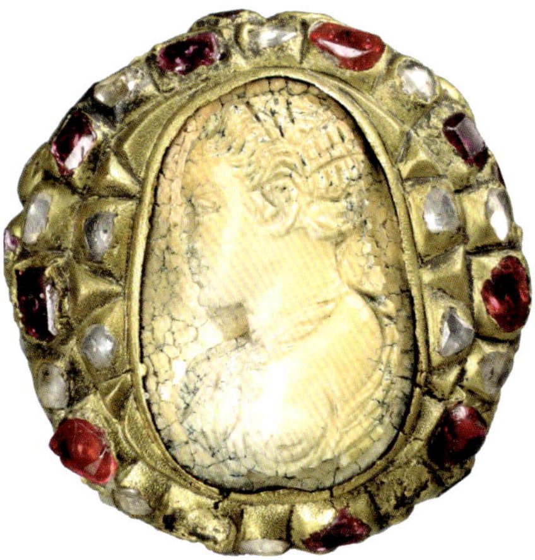

REBUILDING A CITY

On the day of the earthquake, Sebastião José de Carvalho e Melo (1699–1782), prime minister to King José I (r. 1750–77) and the future Marquis of Pombal, launched plans for the rebuilding of Lisbon. By December of 1755, the areas destined for reconstruction had already been identified.

The Pombaline plan was to rebuild the lower part of Lisbon in an ambitious programme that involved the destruction of all pre-existing buildings. New streets were organised according to a rigid orthogonal grid, tellingly designed by military engineers rather than architects.

In November 1806, whilst rebuilding work was in progress, Napoleon decreed the Continental Blockade, a measure that closed European ports to English ships. When Portugal refused to follow the order, in August 1807 the French emperor threatened to invade. With the approach of French and Spanish troops, Prince Regent João (the future King João VI, 1767–1826) gathered together about 10,000 people and left for Brazil.

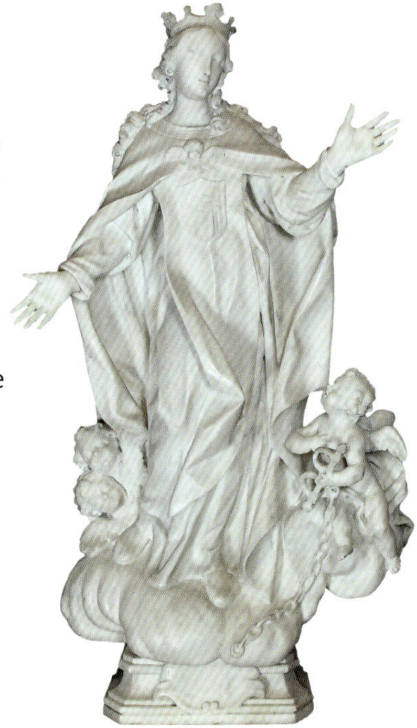

Our Lady of Mercês, mid-/late 18th century
Probably of Italian origin, this marble statue belonged to the chapel of the Pombal Palace in Oeiras, and was likely commissioned by the family of Sebastião José de Carvalho e Melo, Earl of Oeiras and the Marquis of Pombal.

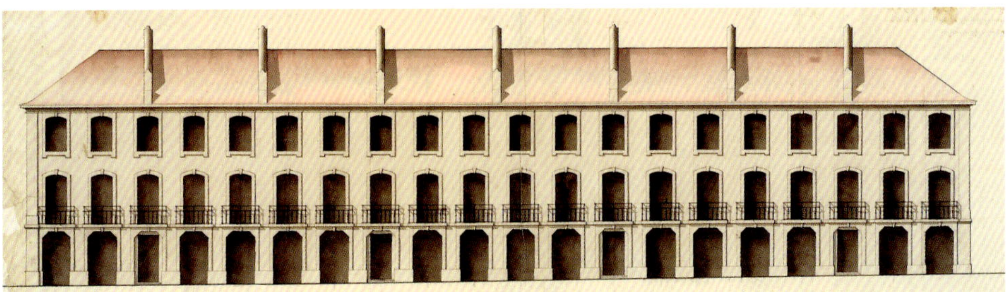

Project no. 1 for the buildings in Baixa, 1756
Eugénio dos Santos e Carvalho
The shape of the Pombaline blocks was incompatible with the pre-earthquake urban grid. Therefore the old, small houses in the downtown area were largely destroyed to allow for the construction of bigger buildings and for the transformation of the urban structure of the city centre.

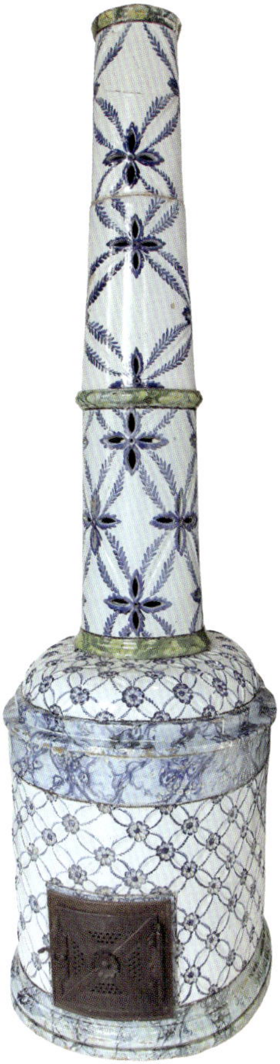

Wood-burning stove, 1790–5
Severino José da Silva
Produced by the Royal Porcelain Factory of Rato (Real Fábrica de Louça do Rato), set up in 1767 under the industrial development policies proposed by the Marquis of Pombal.

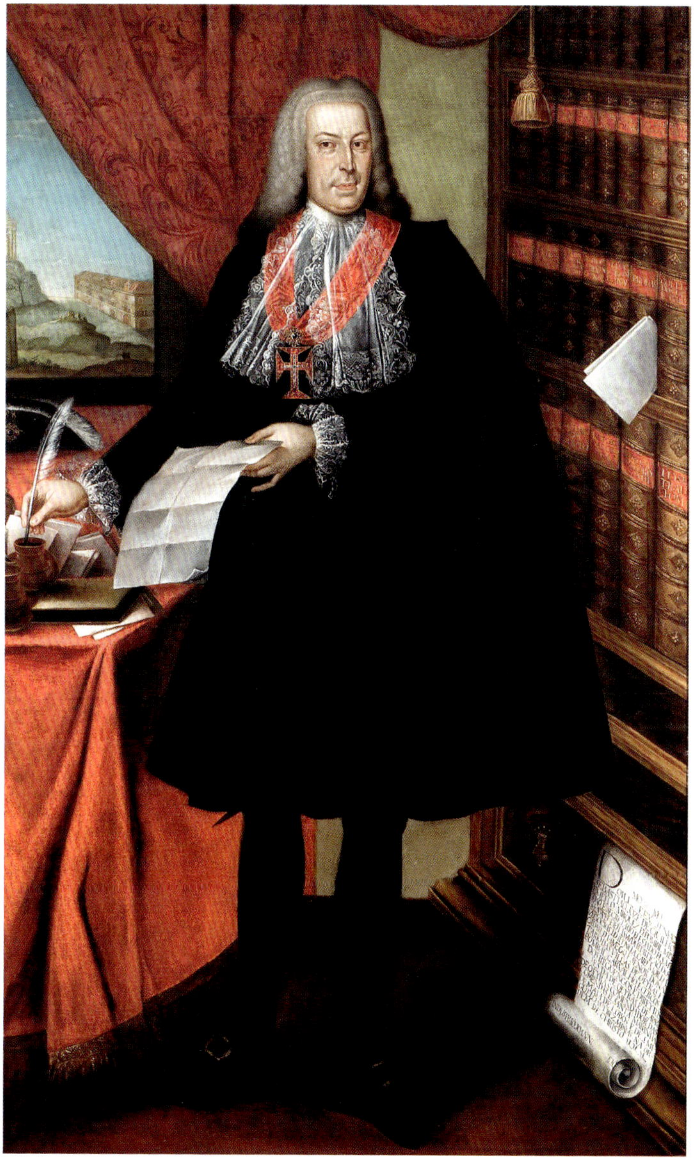

The Marquis of Pombal, late 18th century
Joana do Salitre (D. Joanna Ignacia Monteiro de Carvalho) (attributed)

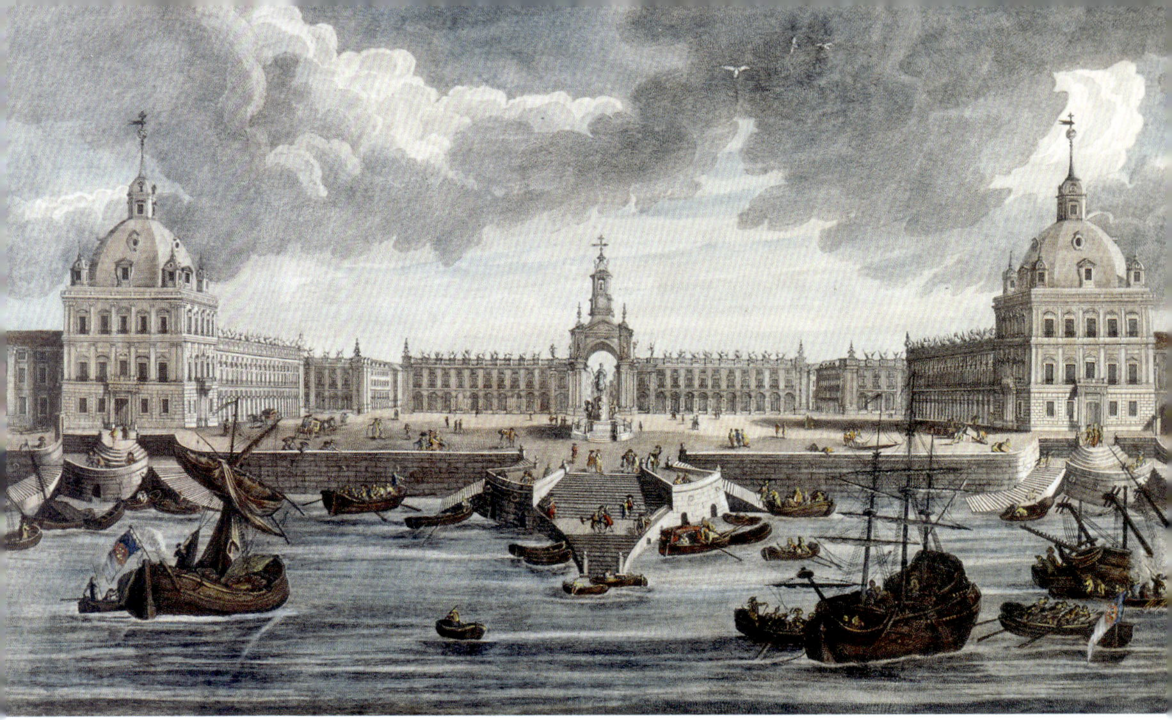

***Praça do Comércio in the city of Lisbon*, late 18th century**
Gaspar Fróis Machado
The old Terreiro do Paço was redesigned and expanded into a symmetrical square, and renamed Praça do Comércio. A monumental symbol of the economic power of the new bourgeois class, it was regarded as the urban centre of the new city, supplanting the popular Rossio.

***Rua Augusta in Lisbon*, 1841–2**
Alexandre de Michellis
The reconstruction of Lisbon took precedence over the paving of the streets. Many mud streets and cobbled pavements remained until almost a century after the earthquake.

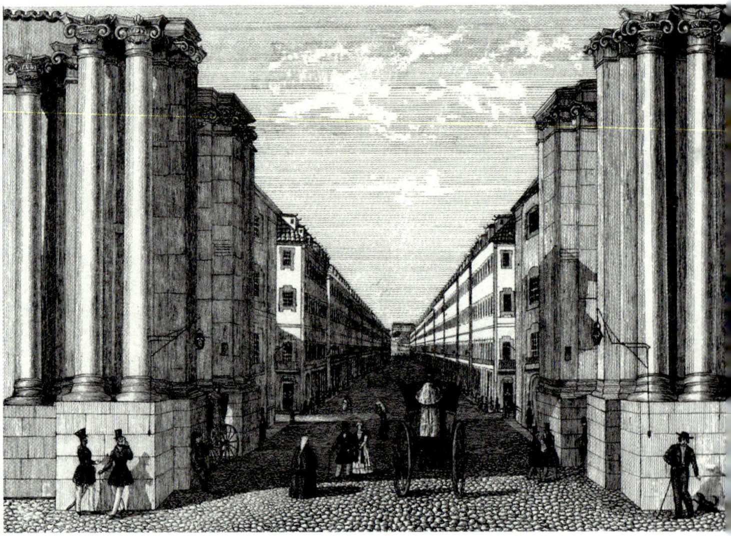

RIGHT: ***Departure of his Royal Highness the Prince Regent of Portugal*, 1815**
Henry L'Évêque (drawing)
Francesco Bartolozzi (engraving)
The royal family departed from Belém two days before the French troops arrived in the capital, commanded by General Junot. Following careful preparations, the prince was accompanied by the court and the entire administrative and bureaucratic apparatus of the State.

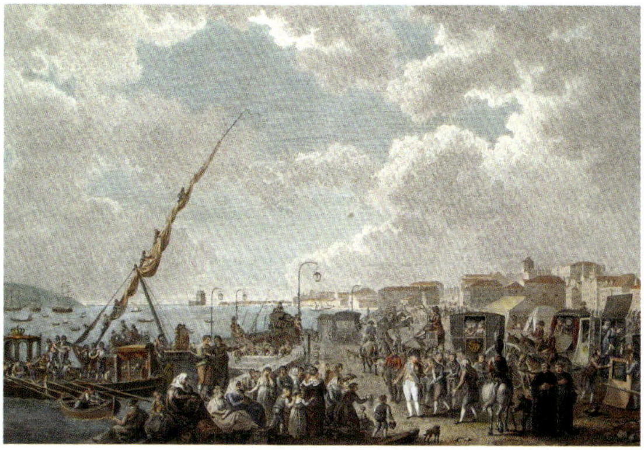

BELOW: ***Royal Palace of Ajuda and the mouth of the River Tagus*, 1871**
Isaias Newton
After the earthquake, the court was moved to Ajuda, an area which had been less affected. Work on the new royal palace began in 1796, to an innovative and grand plan based on the Caserta Palace in Naples.

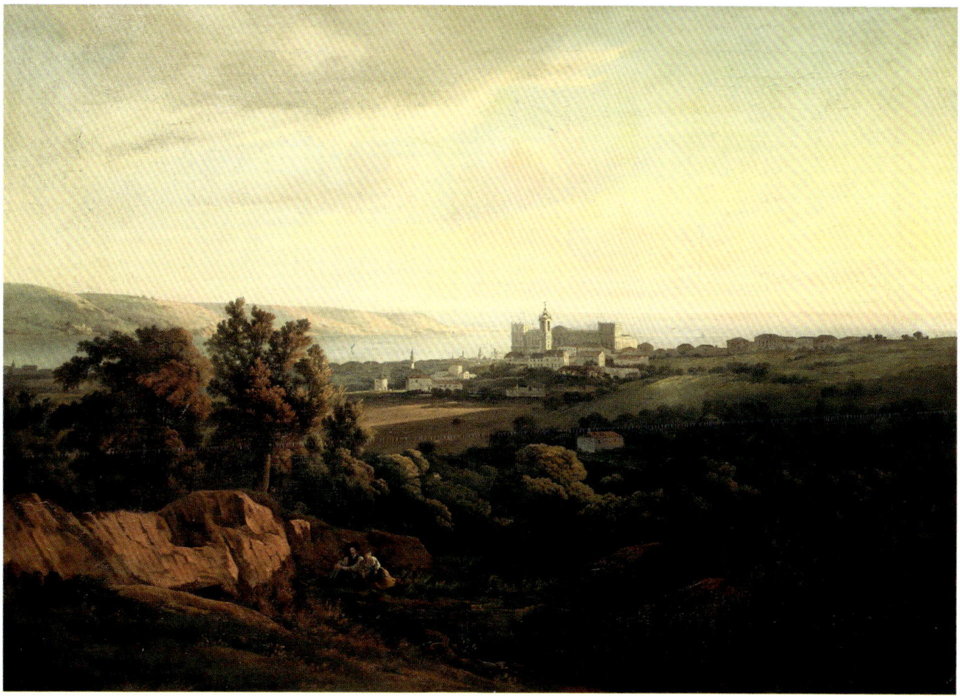

AN EXPANDING CITY

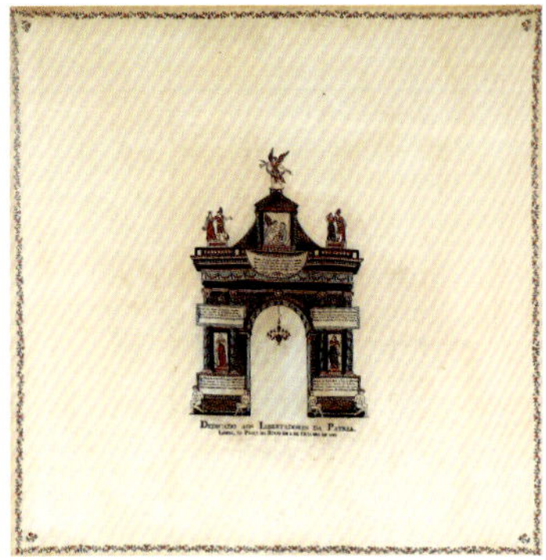

Scarf, 19th century
This silk scarf illustrates the propagandist element of the meeting held in Lisbon on 1 October 1820 (see below). The triumphal arch was in fact built in Rossio Square. It contained a niche with the royal effigy of King João VI (who was in Brazil at the time), swearing the 1822 Liberal Constitution of the kingdom.

During the first half of the nineteenth century, urban regeneration in Lisbon was slow due to a number of factors: instability following the Peninsular Wars, the relocation of the royal court to Brazil, the civil war between the liberals and the absolutists, and the dissolution of religious orders in 1834.

However, between 1851 and 1868, a period of prosperity which became known as the Regeneration led to some significant developments, including gas lighting, the Boavista embankment and the opening of the Estrada da Circunvalação, the ring road circling the city.

More signs of modern urbanisation were evident from the 1870s onwards. Ressano Garcia, the Council's building engineer, drew up plans for the city to grow northwards. The streets that formed part of his plan, known as Avenidas Novas (the New Avenues), drew the city away from its traditional riverside location, but retained the orthogonal layout of the Pombaline reconstruction. The railway was built on landfill sites along the banks of the Tagus, imposing a physical barrier between the inhabitants and the river. The population increased considerably due to industrialisation, and specific districts and workers' neighbourhoods were formed.

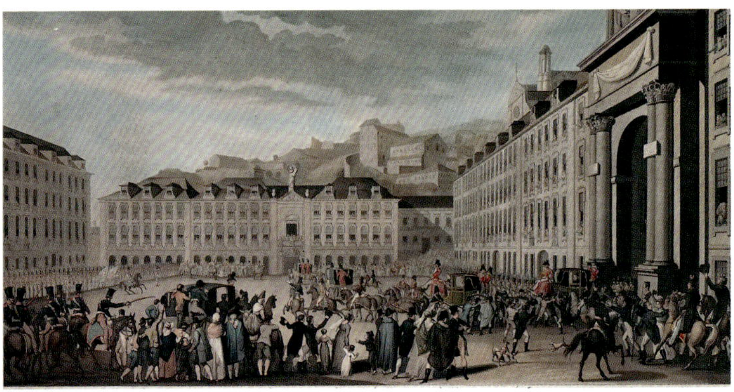

The magnificent and memorable meeting of the illustrious members of the Provisional Council, c.1820
António Cândido Cordeiro Pinheiro Furtado
On 1 October 1820 the members of the Provisional Council of the Supreme Government of the Kingdom met in Lisbon, their intention being to attempt to put an end to the status of Portugal as a colony, since the royal family had remained in Brazil since 1807 and the Kingdom was ruled by English governors.

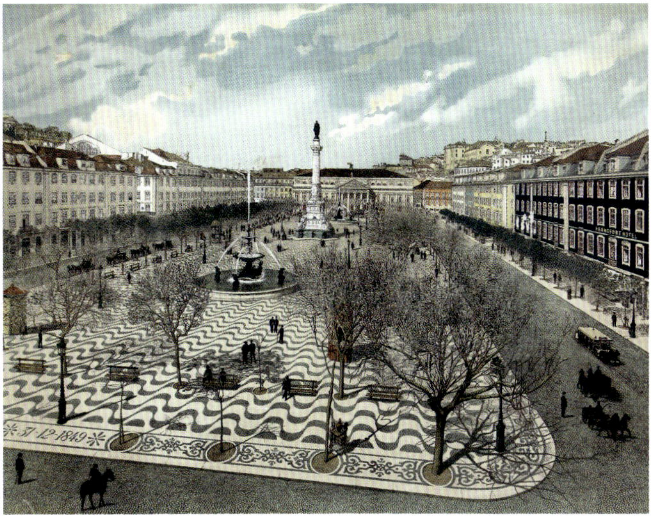

***King Pedro IV Square*, 1849**
In April 1848 the City Council approved the paving of the central part of Rossio Square with cobblestones, following the mosaic-pavement model which would become known as *calçada portuguesa*.

***Former tobacco factory, Xabregas*, 1859**
João Gomes da Silva Pedrozo
The convent of St Francis of Xabregas had a varied history after the suppression of the religious orders in 1834. First it housed the Lisbon Company of Textiles and Spinning, after which it was transformed into a tobacco factory.

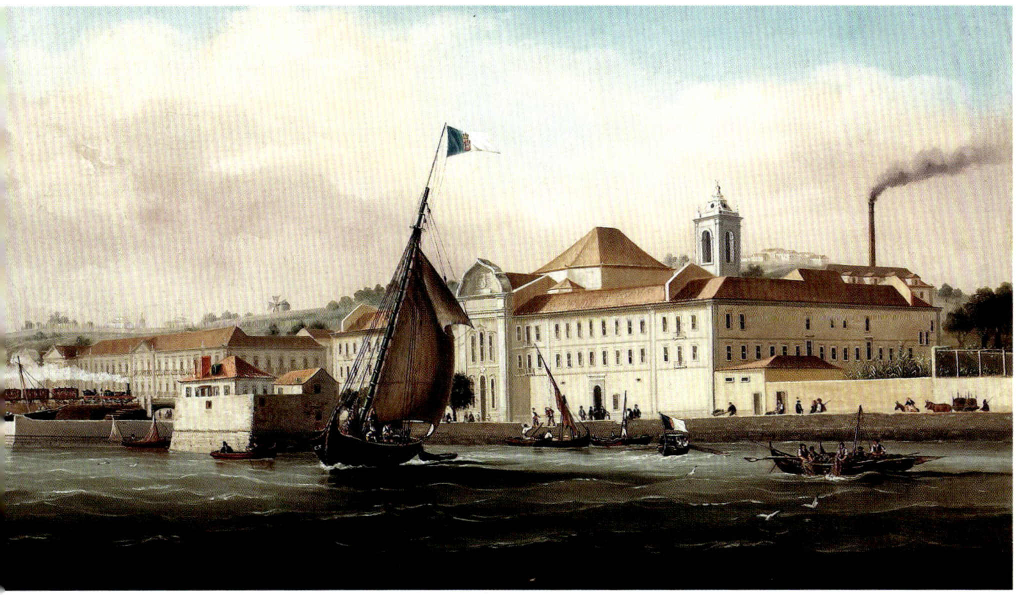

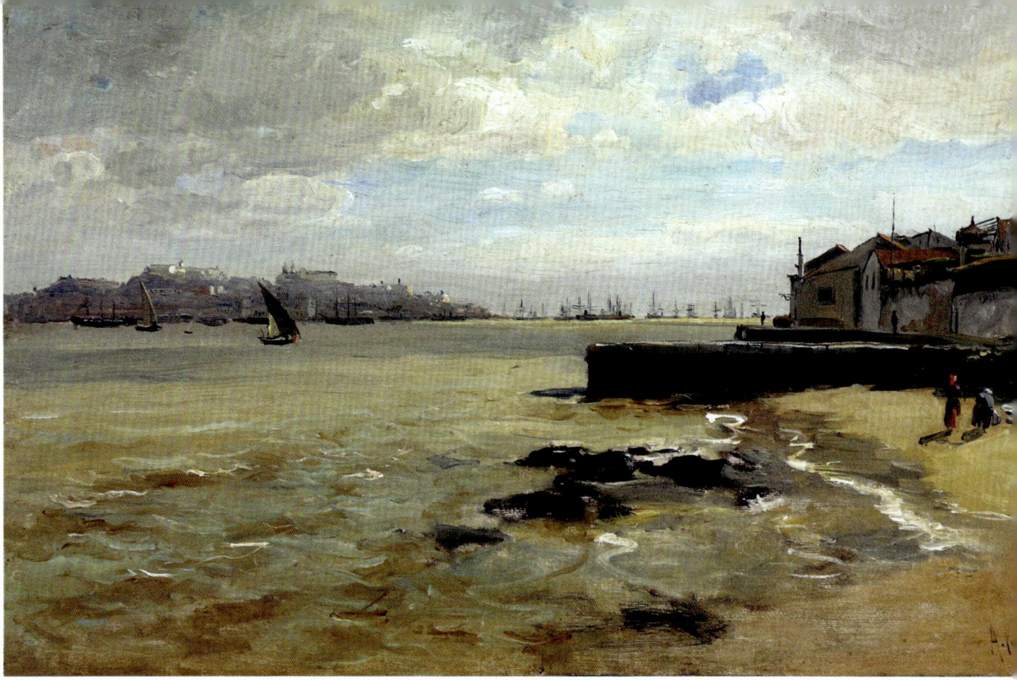

***Lisbon viewed from Ginjal*, mid-/late 19th century**
Alfredo Cristiano Keil

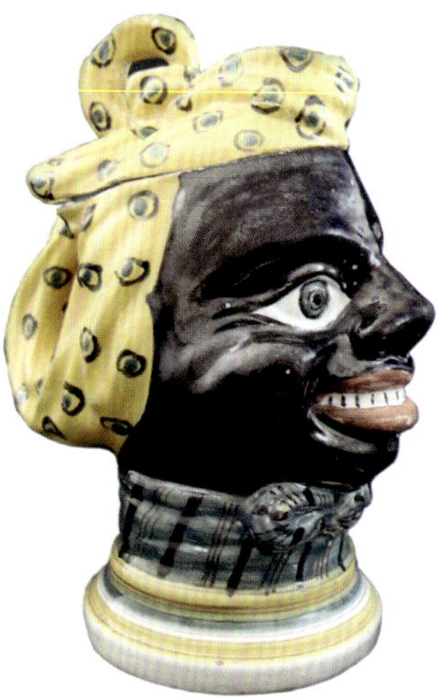

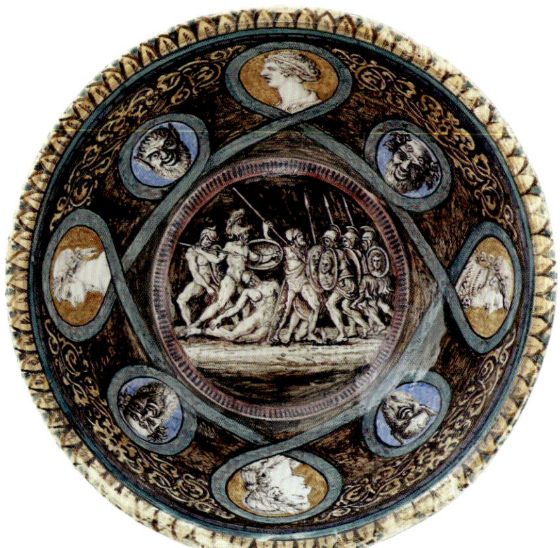

The city of Lisbon protects victims of the French invasion, 1812
Domingos António Sequeira
The painting is on show at Lisbon City Hall.

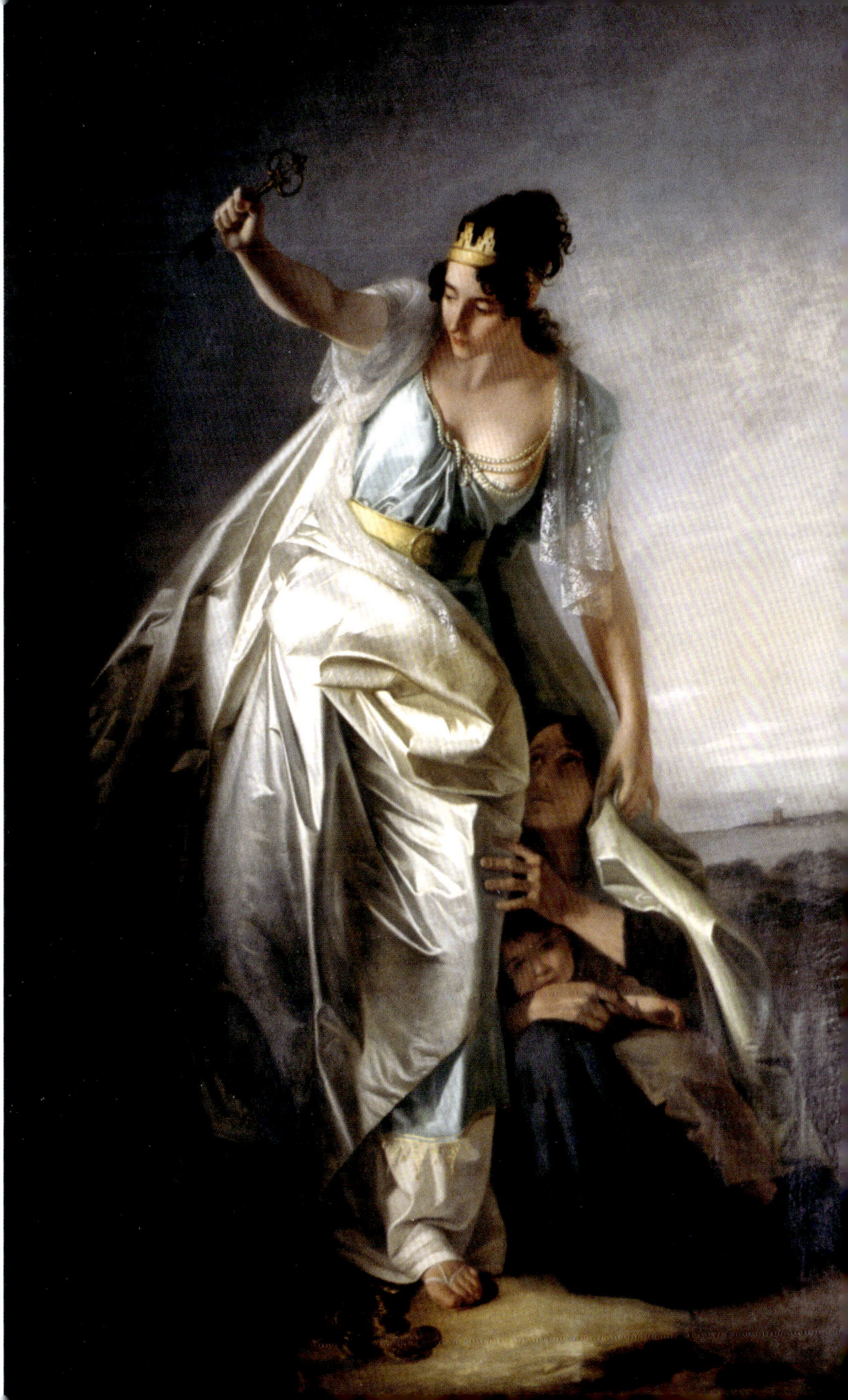

OPPOSITE LEFT:
Tobacco jar, 19th century
This piece depicts a stereotypical image of the African woman, with whom the population of Lisbon shared their daily lives until the abolition of slavery in 1869. Many of these women had responsibilities in the families they worked for, raising children and providing company to the ladies of the house.

OPPOSITE RIGHT:
Bowl, *c.*1870
Wenceslau Cifka
This decorative piece demonstrates the influence of Italian Renaissance majolica in Cifka's work. Showing revivalist characteristics, it is in the romanticist style of the late nineteenth century.

UNDER SALAZAR'S REGIME

On 1 February 1908 King Carlos (r. 1889–1908) and his heir, Prince Luís Filipe, were assassinated, and in November of that year the Portuguese Republican Party won the municipal elections in Lisbon. When the First Republic was established on 5 October 1910, it heralded a period of great social, political and economic upheaval. In the space of 16 years, the regime had 7 parliaments, 8 presidents and 46 governments.

With the installation, on 28 May 1926, of a military dictatorship and the establishment of the Estado Novo (the New State) in the 1933 constitution, the state became a repressive one. The conservative and authoritarian ideology of the regime, under António de Oliveira Salazar, exalted nationalist historical identity and hosted a series of celebrations and commemorations that culminated in the Portuguese World Exhibition of 1940. The event was conceived to affirm Portugal's standing in the modern world, a world at war in which Portugal remained neutral.

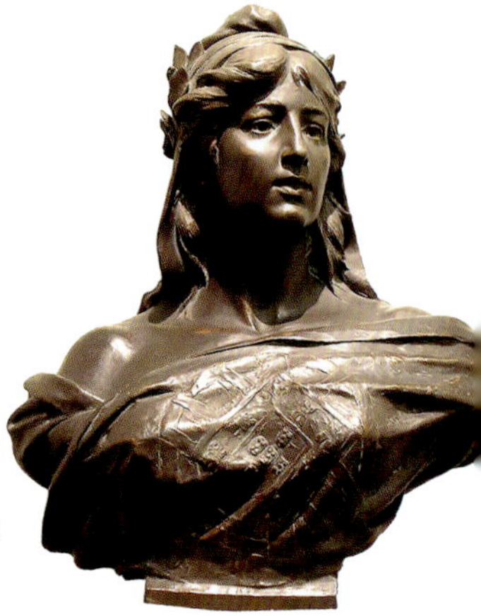

Bust of the Republic, 1911
Simões de Almeida
In 1908 the Republican councillor of Lisbon City Council commissioned the sculptor Simões de Almeida (nephew) to make a female bust to represent the Republic. The style echoed the aesthetic of the French Republic: a young, expressive and exuberant female figure with her hair partially covered by a Phrygian cap.

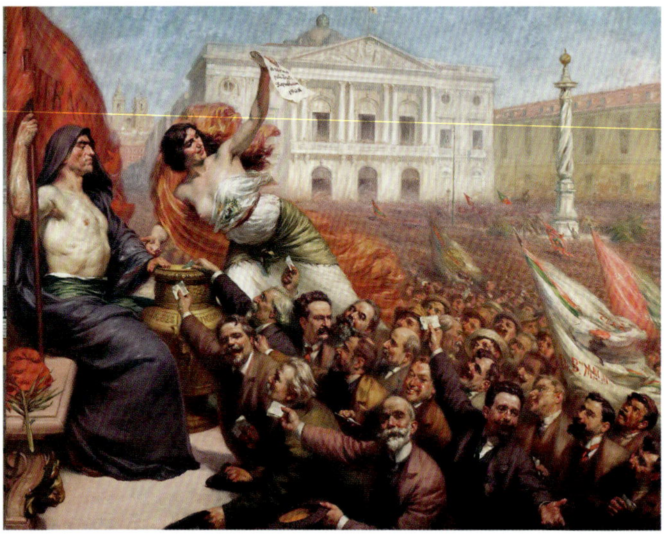

***Suffrage*, 1913**
José Maria Veloso Salgado
In 1912 Lisbon City Council commissioned a painting representing the city electing its first Republican councillors. The setting is the Praça do Município. Pushed forward by a crowd holding banners and flags defending the Republican cause, a group of prominent Republican figures stands out in the foreground to symbolise their status as leaders of the winning Republican movement.

In 1960, thanks to decades of industrial development, which had attracted great numbers of the rural population to the city, Lisbon had over 800,000 inhabitants, a number which continued to increase until the 1980s. This influx of people led to the construction of numerous slums, which social housing policies did nothing to remedy.

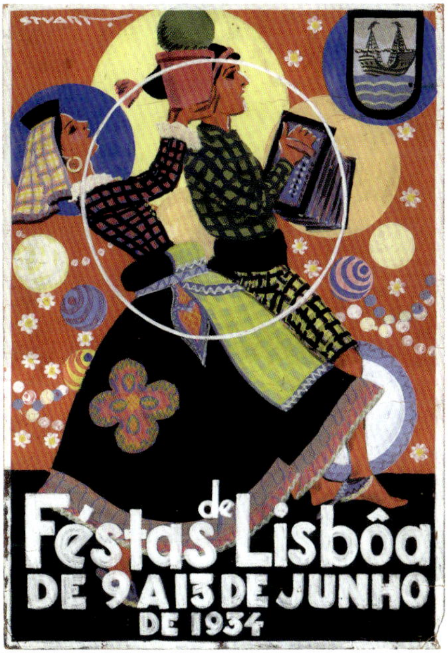

Lisbon Festivals, 1934
Stuart Carvalhais
In 1931, 13 June was made a municipal holiday. The 1934 celebrations consisted of five days of festivities and led to renewed interest in traditional aspects of city life. Popular street parades were instigated in the same year, a festive tradition that continues today.

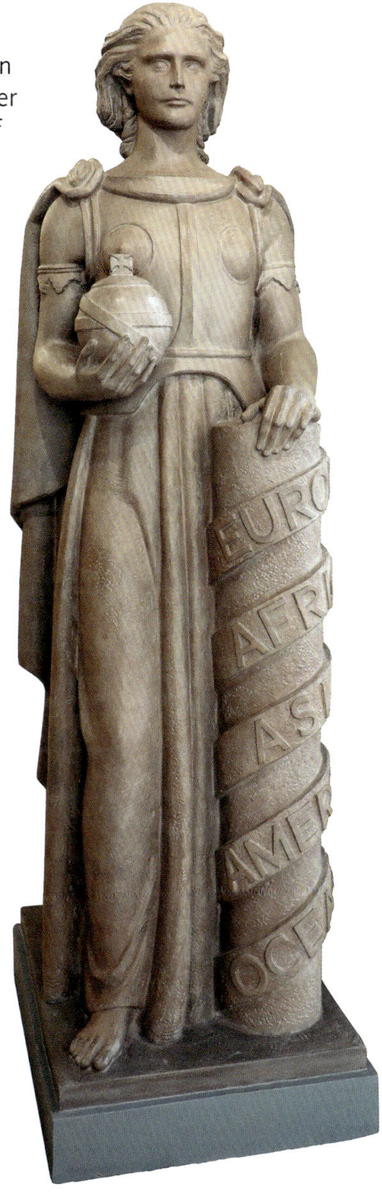

Sovereignty, 1939
Leopoldo de Almeida
The Portuguese World Exhibition began on 23 June 1940, only a few days after German troops occupied Paris. The event commemorated two 'glorious' dates for the regime's ideology: the double centenary of the foundation of Portugal (1140) and the restoration of Portuguese independence (1640). This statue, an allegory to Portuguese sovereignty, was placed in a prominent position to welcome visitors to the Exhibition.

RIGHT:

***O fado*, 1910**

José Malhoa

This painting was inspired by the artist's visits to fado houses and taverns in the Mouraria district in search of bohemian figures and marginal environments. Fado, a unique form of popular urban music originating in the nineteenth century, is on UNESCO's World's Intangible Cultural Heritage list. The painting is on show at the Fado Museum.

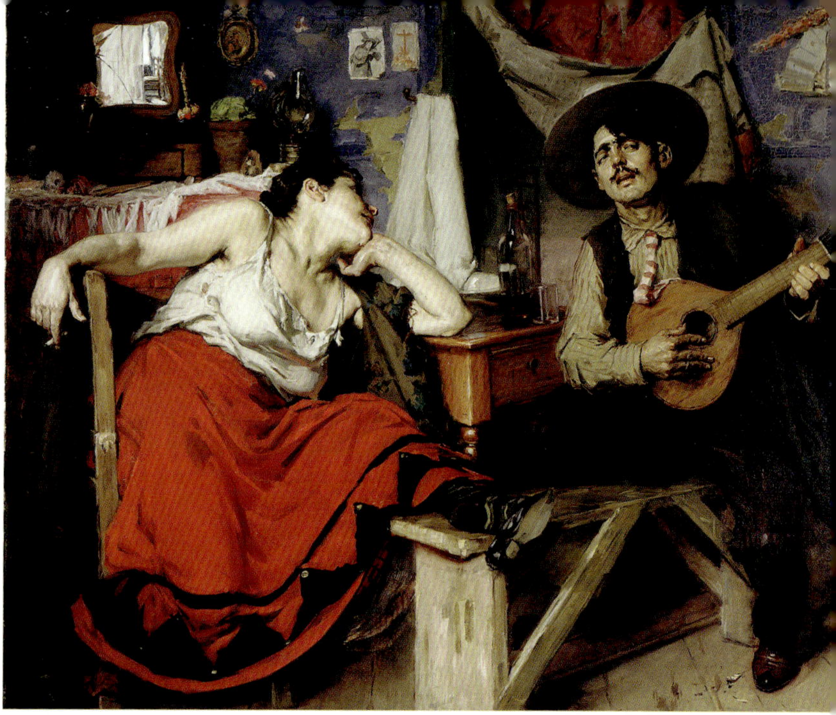

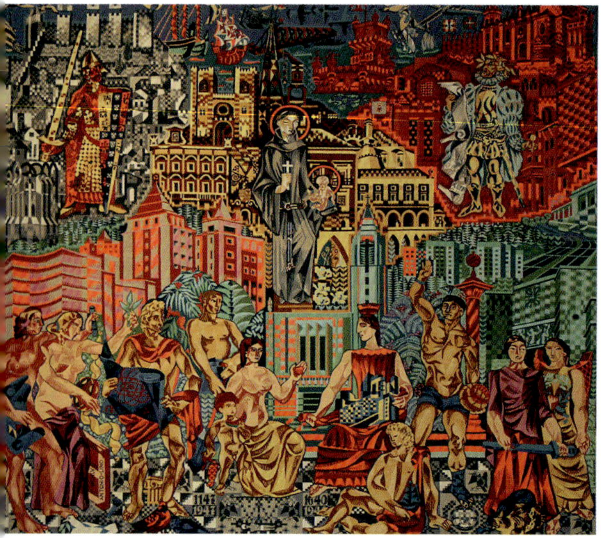

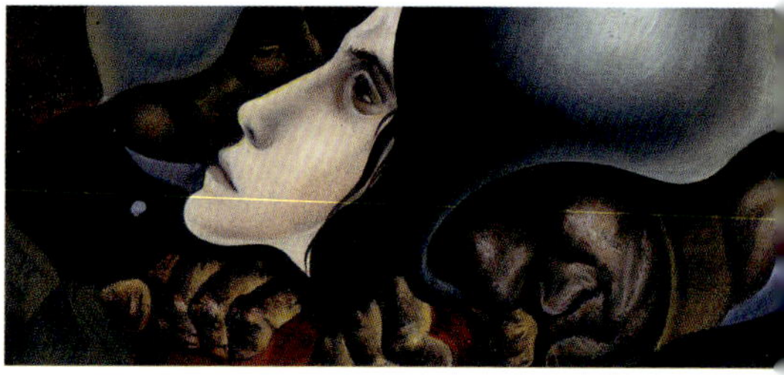

LEFT:

***Glory of Lisbon*, 1955**

Lino António

Illustrating historical figures and buildings of the city from the Middle Ages to the twentieth century, this tapestry was commissioned by Lisbon City Council. It is one of the most expressive tapestries of Salazar's regime (Estado Novo).

ABOVE:

***Resistance*, 1946**

Júlio Pomar

This neo-realistic painting is of great significance in Portugal. With a young prisoner between two soldiers, it represents resistance to Totalitarianism. The painting is on show at Júlio Pomar's Atelier-Museum.

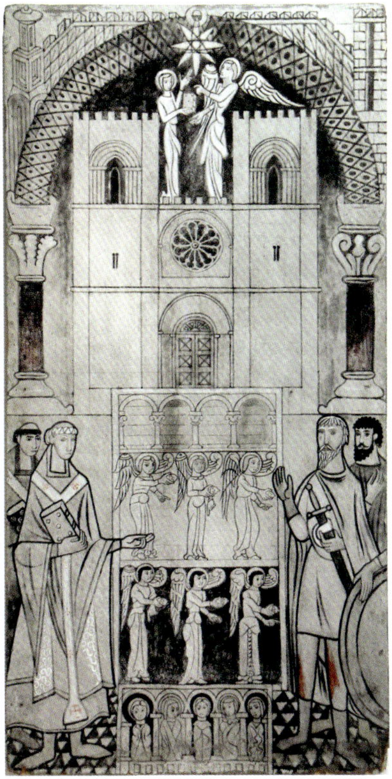

BELOW:
***Camões*, c.1932**
António Soares
This painting reflects how the modernist painter António Soares envisioned Luís Vaz de Camões (1524–1580), the Portuguese poet: restless, theatrical and entangled in his own thoughts.

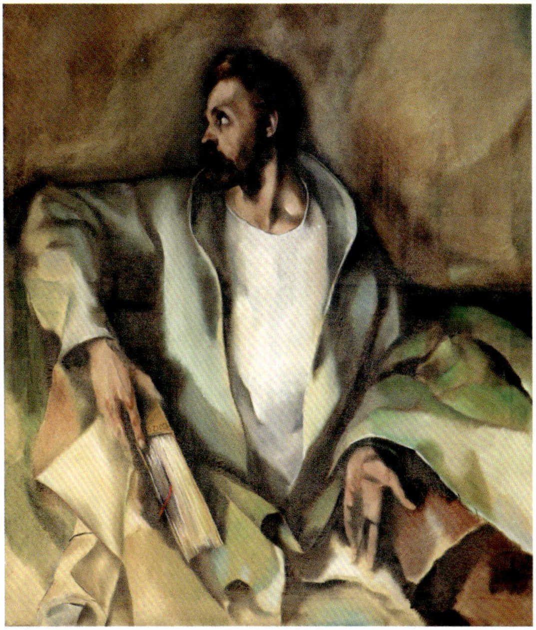

ABOVE:
***Sé Catedral de Lisboa*, 1947**
Almada Negreiros
Conceived for the 800th anniversary of the Lisbon Siege (1147), this piece depicts the façade of Lisbon Cathedral, among other medieval elements.

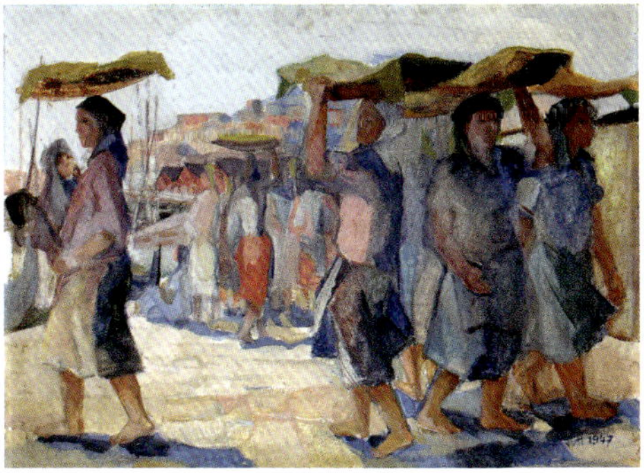

LEFT:
***Cais do Sodré*, 1947**
Hansi Stäel
For decades the fishwife was a symbol of Lisbon, because of her connection to the river and the colour and character she brought to the city. Her uninhibited and irreverent nature attracted the attention of artists, journalists, writers and photographers.

CONTEMPORARY LISBON

The democratic regime that emerged after the revolution of 25 April 1974 continued to struggle with the housing problem in Lisbon, especially in the suburbs. In the city centre, work on historic neighbourhoods was slow, and it was only in the late 1980s that local organisations were set up in Alfama and Mouraria to address housing issues.

The 1990s were challenging years for the city. In 1993 the Special Rehabilitation Plan was implemented, which aimed to demolish the slums and provide accommodation for people in low-rise buildings. The 1994 Municipal Master Plan led to the creation of some iconic buildings in the city, including Centro Cultural de Belém (The Belém Cultural Center) in 1992. Lisbon also hosted Expo '98 (the 1998 Lisbon World Exposition), which was an opportunity to rejuvenate the eastern side of the city, which had until then been something of an industrial wasteland.

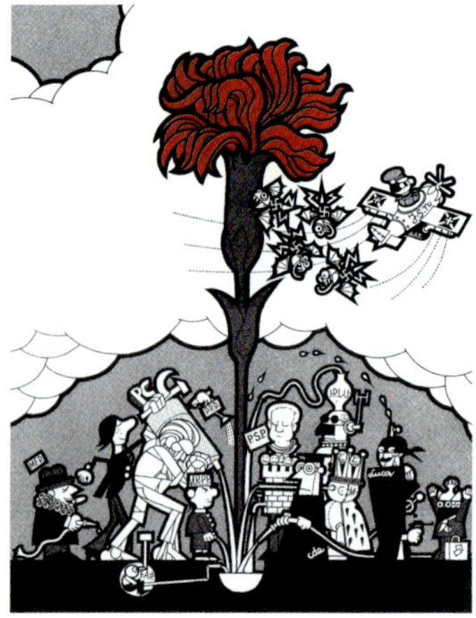

***Red carnation of the revolution*, 1974**
João Abel Manta
This drawing is from soon after the revolution of 25 April 1974. The giant carnation symbolises freedom. It flourishes thanks to the perseverance of the democratic political forces that water it, oblivious to the far-right threat represented by a Nazi plane dropping 'insect-bombs' which try to devour it.

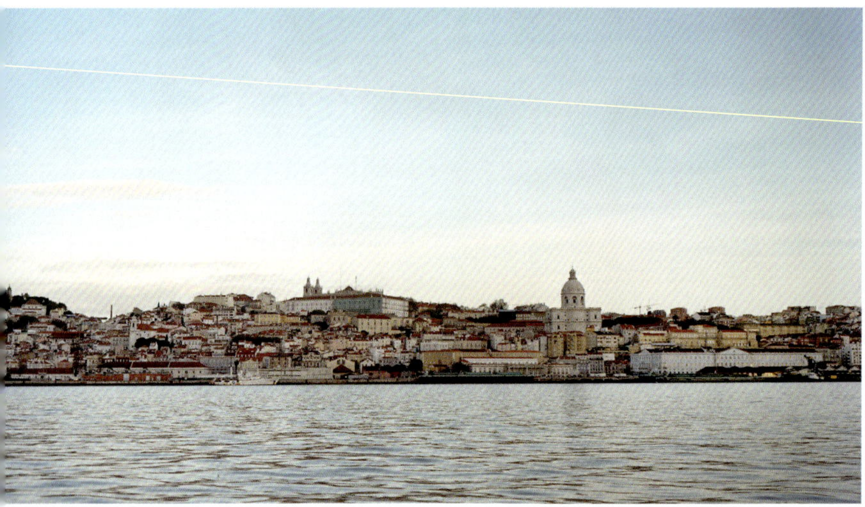

***Earth (Tagus #1)*, 2008**
Nuno Cera
This view of the eastern part of Lisbon today illustrates the relationship of the city with the Tagus River. It is one of a series of photographs featuring Portuguese cities connected to rivers.

***Houses of Lisbon*, 1986**
Paulo Ossião
Through the overlapping of buildings, including the cathedral, the painter reveals the topography of the historic city centre with its traditional houses, in contrast to the contemporary city that was emerging at the time.

***The Tower of Belém*, 1992**
Querubim Lapa
This panel of checkered tiles simulating a staircase shows the Tower of Belém between two palm trees at the top.

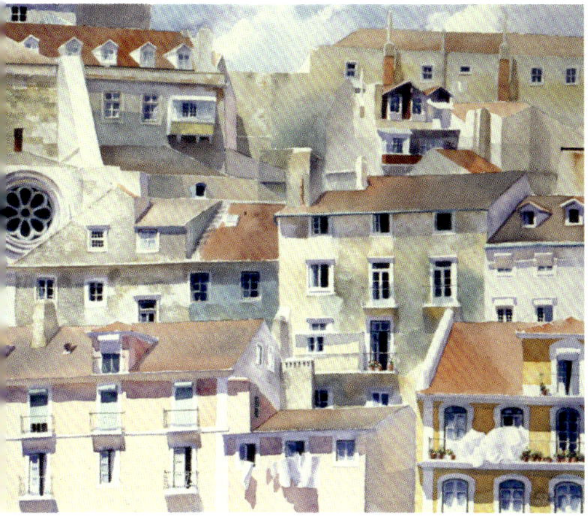

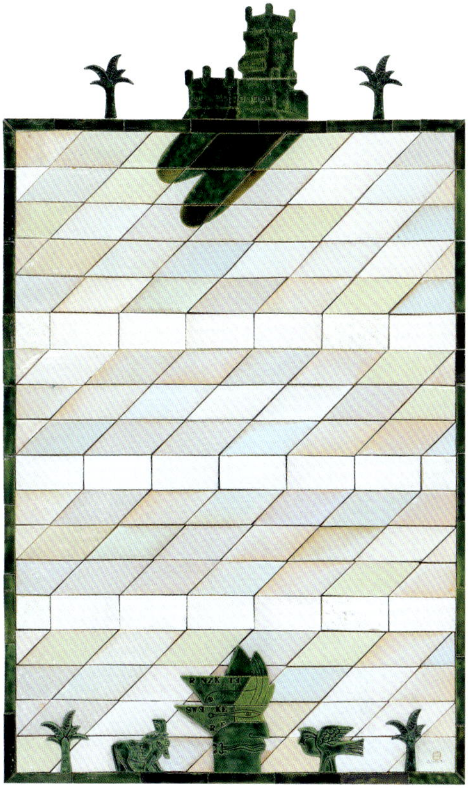

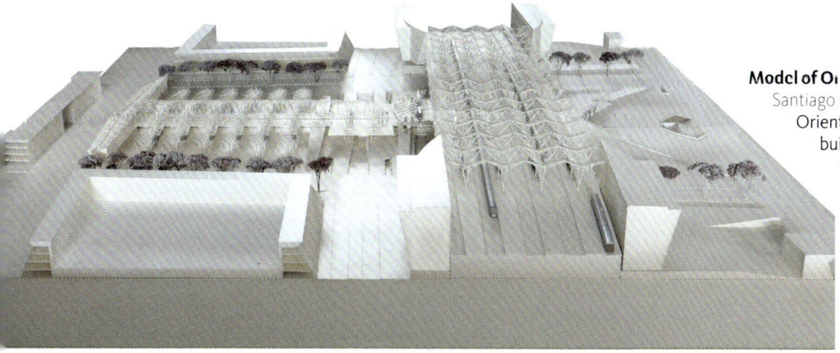

Model of Oriente train station, 1994
Santiago Calatrava (architect)
Oriente Station is an iconic building from Expo '98, and the main intermodal station of the city today. It was a key element in the urban rejuvenation for Expo '98, which led to the development of the neighbourhood of Parque das Nações.

First published in 2020 by
Scala Arts & Heritage Publishers Ltd
10 Lion Yard
Tremadoc Road
London SW4 7NQ, UK
www.scalapublishers.com

In association with the Museum of Lisbon
www.museudelisboa.pt/en

ISBN: 978 1 78551 258 2

Project editor: Sandra Pisano
Designer: Nigel Soper
Printed and bound in Turkey

10 9 8 7 6 5 4 3 2 1

INSIDE FRONT COVER:
Model of Lisbon before the 1755 earthquake, 1950s
Gustavo de Matos Sequeira, Ticiano Violante, Jaime Martins Barata
Set up on 17 boards, the city is represented on the eve of the disaster, between Alcântara and Santa Apolónia, and between the River Tagus and a line to the north drawn slightly beyond Rato and Senhora do Monte. The model has been exhibited in Pimenta Palace since 1982.

INSIDE BACK COVER:
Topographical map of the City of Lisbon/copy of plan No. 5 (Map of the City of Lisbon – Baixa), 1898
Original by Eugénio dos Santos and Carlos Mardel, copy by Augusto Vieira da Silva
This plan for the reconstruction of Lisbon, dated April 1756 and sealed by decree in June 1758, shows the layout of the city before the earthquake (marked in pink) and the overlap of the plans for rebuilding (marked in yellow). It was chosen from among six proposals, and was the most radical. It favoured symmetry and proportionality between blocks, with no diagonal roads.

Expo '98 model of Parque das Nações and the surrounding urban area, 1995–8
Portugal dos Pequeninos
Marking the 500th anniversary of the discovery of the sea route to India, the main theme of Expo '98 was 'The Oceans: A Heritage for the Future'. About 150 countries participated and there were five large thematic pavilions.

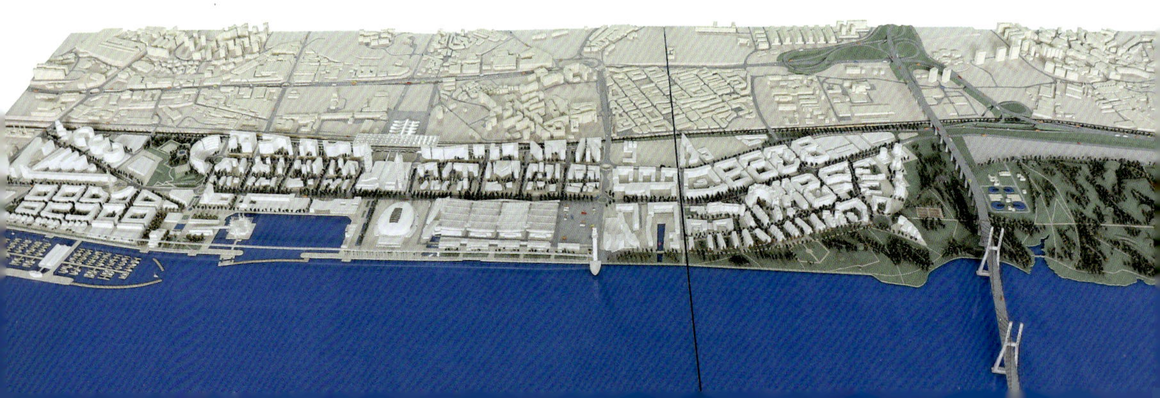